Meet Mary

Mark Miravalle

Meet Mary

Getting to Know
the Mother of God

SOPHIA INSTITUTE PRESS®
Manchester, New Hampshire

Sophia Institute Press
Box 5284, Manchester, NH 03108
1-800-888-9344
www.SophiaInstitute.com

Sophia Institute Press® is a registered trademark of Sophia Institute.

Library of Congress Cataloging-in-Publication Data

Miravalle, Mark I., 1959-
    Meet Mary : getting to know the mother of God /
    Mark Miravalle.
        p. cm.
    Includes bibliographical references.
    ISBN 978-1-933184-32-6 (pbk. : alk. paper)
    1. Mary, Blessed Virgin, Saint. I. Title.

BT603.M57 2007
232.91 — dc22
                                          2007042897

To my mother,
to my wife,
and to all mothers
who heroically bear
and nurture God's images

Contents

Special thanks to Emily Stimpson and Todd Aglialoro for their astute editorial efforts in "translating" my Mariological thoughts into plain English

Not Just a Catholic Thing

A book about Mary, written by a Catholic theologian, that can be read by non-Catholics and non-Christians? I can just see the eyebrows rising and hear the questions forming.

"Why on earth should non-Catholics and non-Christians read a book about Mary anyway?" "What is this book all about?" "Why is this man writing this book?" "Who is he anyway?"

With those questions ever present in my mind as I undertake this little book, I thought perhaps I might begin by providing some answers right up front. So, in reverse order . . .

Who am I?

In addition to being the father of eight and the husband of one, I am, as I already mentioned, a Catholic theologian. And not just a Catholic theologian, but a Catholic theologian who specializes in writing and teaching about Jesus' mother. I'm what Catholics call a "Mariologist," which literally translates into "one who studies Mary." Importantly, for me at least, I believe what I teach. I am a card-carrying, Rosary-praying Catholic.

Why am I writing this book?

My reasons are pretty simple. Over the past few years, there has been an increasing amount of attention given to Mary, both by the secular press and by people who are decidedly not Catholic. *Time* magazine ran a cover story on Marian devotion, *Dateline NBC* did a one-hour special on Marian miracles, and even the Protestant standard *Christianity Today* featured a series of articles on Mary, including one titled, "The Blessed Evangelical Mary: Why We Shouldn't Ignore Her Any Longer." Venerable Protestant pastors such as the Rev. John Buchanan of Fourth Presbyterian Church in Chicago have started preaching sermons about her, and young Christian authors such as Shannon Kubiak have started writing books about her. Radical feminists are holding her up as a model of female empowerment, and Muslims do homage to her on a daily basis.

When you have all these people talking and writing about someone about whom most non-Catholics know little, people start asking questions. "What does Mary have to do with my relationship with God?" "What does the Bible tell us about her?" And my personal favorite: "Why do Catholics worship Mary?"

Probably because the job title next to my name is "Mariologist," I've found that people like to come to me for answers to such questions. And so I thought I might simplify the whole process by just handing people a book that answers the questions for me!

In all seriousness, the number of people with questions about Mary does seem to grow by leaps and bounds with each passing year, and that is why I've sat down to write this book — to give them a sure and ready source for good answers.

Which brings me to the next question: what is this book all about — and what is it not about? Let's start with the latter.

First, this book is not a piece of apologetics. In other words, I'm not trying to convince non-Catholics and non-Christians to accept some or all of the Church's beliefs about Mary. Obviously, I think it would be great if they did, since I happen to hold that everything that follows in these pages is true, and subscribing to what is true is always a good thing. My personal feelings aside, however, converting readers is not the direct point of this book.

Next, this book is not a biography of Mary. It doesn't aim to piece together the life of the mother of Christ by filling in the biblical blanks with bits from the apocrypha or my imagination. Neither am I advancing some political or religious agenda. This book is not a Feminist, Marxist, Zionist, or any other kind of "-ist" reconstruction of Mary. There are no "-ists" in this book.

Finally, this book is not a watered-down, ecumenical rendition of Catholic teaching. It doesn't leave out those parts of the Church's beliefs that non-Catholics and non-Christians will find difficult or even repugnant. It doesn't look for common ground, although you'll find a great deal of that in any case.

This book *is* a straightforward presentation of Catholic teaching on Mary — where we encounter her in the Bible, what core beliefs we hold about her, how we honor her, and how she honors us in return — with the goal of leading you to a personal encounter with an extraordinary woman who lived two thousand years ago and lives still today. It's a sort of Marian guidebook for inquiring minds who want to know: who want to know *about* Mary, and who want to *know* Mary.

And that is the answer to why non-Catholics and non-Christians should read a book about Mary written by a Catholic.

The Catholic Church has spent the past two millennia getting to know the mother of Jesus. We've studied her in Scripture, contemplated her in prayer, and honored her in our liturgies. We've tried to see the face of Jesus through her eyes — eyes that watched him in the manger, in the Temple, and on the Cross. John Paul II called this kind of contemplation "studying at the school of Mary."

Unfortunately, there have been, over the course of those millennia, those who focused more on the teacher than on what she taught. At rare times, Catholics and non-Catholics alike have succumbed to Marian excess, giving Jesus' mother honors and devotions that she does not seek and does not want — indeed, that she finds offensive. I want to make it clear up front that those who adore or worship her as semi-divine, or who even place her on the level of the Trinity, are not living out the Catholic Church's teachings. Neither are those who let acts of honor become superstitious rituals. Treating Mary like a goddess or a magician is strictly *verboten* in the Catholic Church.

But so is ignoring her.

Through the centuries, the vast majority of Catholics have managed to walk the very wide road between Marian excess and Marian neglect. They have said their Hail Marys, asked for her prayers, and named their daughters Mary Ann, Mary Margaret, and Mary Catherine. They have loved her as they love their own mother, striving to follow her example in faith, love, and obedience. They have, as Jesus commissioned the apostle John, taken her into their own homes.

And in return, they found a woman who understands suffering, who knows what it's like to follow God at the risk of losing all, even what she loves most in all the world. They found a heart that has grieved, yet never ceased to believe. They found a mother. Even more important, they found Christ. And that is the true heart of all Marian devotion: coming to know and love Christ more deeply and more truly.

∞

Mary was born to bring Jesus into the world. God, who we believe knows all things from before the beginning of time, knew when he created her what role she would play in salvation history.[1] And when she uttered her yes to the angel Gabriel, she began that work he predestined for her. Catholics believe she continues that work even today, bringing Christ to souls and souls to Christ. And so it really is all about *him*. All the Rosaries, all the statues, all the Mary Margarets running about in Catholic-school jumpers — they are, ultimately, all about honoring Christ.

That's why getting to know Mary, the mother of Jesus, is so important for all Christians, including those who don't look to the Roman gentleman in white as their earthly spiritual father. And why, to perhaps an even greater degree, having more than a passing acquaintance with Mary is necessary for the non-Christian wanting to understand the Christian faith or looking for a model of love and compassion. Just as getting to know your spouse's mother will help you know your spouse all the more, so, too, will getting to know Jesus' mother help you to know him all the more. And while in Mary you will find a supreme model of love and compassion, you will also find that, over time, she will point you to an even better one: Christ himself.

Meet Mary

Chapter One

Be It Done unto Me
Mary in the Bible and the Early Church

So, who is this woman who has had cathedrals named for her, poems written about her, and battles fought in her honor? Who is this Mary?

Of the details of her life, we know little. Much of what we do know was recorded in the pages of the New Testament and passed down through the oral tradition of the early Church. Written on scrolls of parchment and the walls of the catacombs, this history gives only the briefest sketch of the woman who brought Jesus into the world.

The glimpses into her life and character that we do get, however, are rich with significance, which is exactly why millions of men and women through the centuries have found in her a model of holiness, a companion in suffering, and, above all, a mother of their own.

Mary in the New Testament
In the pages of the New Testament, we have the oldest historical record of Mary's life. Almost all that we know of her earthly existence we know from the four Gospels, which were written sometime between 50 and 100 AD, along with the oral tradition passed on by the first Christians.

Meet Mary

We know she was raised in Galilee, one of the most remote corners of one of the most remote provinces of the ancient Roman Empire. We know that when she came along in approximately 14 BC, Israel was governed by Herod, a sadistic and power-hungry king who ruled at the pleasure of the emperor in Rome. A representative of that emperor, the governor, also sat in Jerusalem, supervising the soldiers, keeping an eye on Herod, and putting down the periodic rebellions that sprang up among the Jewish people.

We also know that Mary was Jewish, a member of a people that had been persecuted, enslaved, exiled, and oppressed for thousands of years, yet who continued to worship the God of its ancestors and to reject the polytheism of its oppressors. We know that she married a carpenter named Joseph, gave birth to a son named Jesus, watched her son become a man, and later watched him die on a cross.

The most detailed written information we have on Mary's early life and relationship with her son comes from the Gospel of Luke. Luke, more so than any of the other Gospel writers, was concerned with giving an in-depth history of Jesus' life, so he included more detailed information about Jesus' early years than the others did. In his Gospel, there are five key events in Christ's early life that involve his mother. Here they are, according to their traditional names:

• *The Annunciation,*[2] when the angel Gabriel greets Mary with the words, "Hail, full of grace, the Lord is with you." He then informs her that she will conceive a child, who will go on to become the savior of the world. After asking, "How can this be, since I have no husband," Mary accepts his answer, replying, "Behold, I am the handmaid of the Lord; let it be to me according to your word."

- *The Visitation,*[3] when Mary visits her cousin Elizabeth, the expectant mother of John the Baptist. When Elizabeth first sees Mary, her child leaps in her womb, and Elizabeth cries out, "Blessed are you among women, and blessed is the fruit of your womb!" and Mary proclaims in return, "All generations will call me blessed."

- *The Nativity,*[4] when Mary gives birth to Jesus in a stable and, as the Christmas plays remind us, "wrapped him in swaddling clothes."

- *The Presentation* of the infant Jesus in the Temple by Mary and Joseph, a Jewish ritual duty. There, an old man named Simeon prophesies about Jesus and warns Mary, "A sword will pierce through your own soul also."

- *The Finding of the Child Jesus in the Temple* after he had been lost for three days. When Jesus tells Mary and Joseph that "I must be in my Father's house," we learn that Mary "kept all these things in her heart."

From the Gospel of Matthew, we also learn about:

- *The betrothal of Mary*[5] to Joseph the carpenter.

- *Joseph's confusion* about Mary's pregnancy. When he considers divorcing her quietly, an angel appears to him, saying, "Do not fear to take Mary your wife, for that which is conceived of her is of the Holy Spirit."

- *The arrival of the three Wise Men,*[6] who "going into the house . . . saw the child with Mary his mother, and they fell down and worshiped him."

- *The flight of Jesus' family,*[7] when Joseph is again instructed in a dream to "take the child and his mother, and flee to Egypt."

- *The return to Israel,*[8] when, after Herod the Great's death, an angel once more speaks to Joseph, telling him, "Rise, take the child and his mother, and go to the land of Israel, for those who sought the child's life are dead."

Beyond the infancy narratives in Luke and Matthew, there are five important references to Mary in Scripture:

- *The Wedding at Cana,*[9] where, at Mary's request, Jesus performs his first public miracle — turning water into wine — and begins his active ministry. Mary's words to the servants, "Do whatever he tells you," describe the heart of her message to all believers across time.

- *Mary at the foot of the Cross.*[10] Hanging on the Cross, Jesus says to Mary and to the disciple whom he loved, "Woman, behold, your son . . . Behold, your mother." We also learn that "from that hour, the disciple took her to his own home."

- *The presence of Mary in the Upper Room,*[11] awaiting, with the early disciples of Jesus, the arrival of the Holy Spirit.

- *Paul's reference*[12] to the Savior "born of a woman."

- *John's vision in Revelation,*[13] in which he describes "a woman clothed with the sun, with the moon under her feet, and on her head a crown of twelve stars." He goes on to make it clear that he's referring to Mary, declaring, "She brought forth a male child, one who is to rule all nations with a rod of iron."[14]

John also alludes to the woman's "other offspring . . . those who keep the commandments of God and bear testimony to Jesus."[15]

With one or two exceptions, that is all the New Testament has to say about the mother of Jesus. Yet those few passages, coupled with the oral faith and life of the Church of Jesus and his first apostles and disciples, are the foundation of what the Catholic Church teaches and believes about Mary; the seeds from which fully formed doctrines would emerge. We'll explore the relationship between the seeds and their blossoming fruits in the next chapter, but for now, let's sum up the key Marian themes that emerge in the New Testament.

* *Mary's miraculous motherhood:* Although Mary is really and truly Jesus' mother, she is a mother like no other. The child born of her was conceived virginally; he had no man for a father. So, from the beginning, we get a rather strong indication that Mary's relationship with God was a bit different from most women's (or men's).

* *The unity of the mother and child:* This theme is particularly evident in Matthew, where, in the first chapters, the two are almost never mentioned more than a breath apart.

* *Mary's suffering:* Being the mother of the Christ is no easy job. Her midnight flight into a strange land, the warning of a sword piercing her soul, and her presence at the foot of the Cross while her son dies an agonizing death give us a glimpse of the sorrows she endured in her lifetime.

* *Mary as "Woman":* On two occasions, we hear Mary referred to not by her name or her relationship with her son,

but simply as "Woman." This is not a token of disrespect, but is done expressly to highlight the role she plays in salvation history.

We'll see how, when we explore all of those themes in greater depth in the next chapter. But before we move on to look at Mary's role in the early Church, we need to look backward, to the books of the Old Testament.

Mary in the Old Testament

"The Old Testament?" you ask. "Mary wasn't even born until generations after the last book of the Hebrew Scriptures was written."

To answer that point, I need to explain how Catholics read the Bible. We don't believe that the Old Testament and New Testament are two separate entities, entirely unrelated to each other. Rather, we hold that both were inspired by the same God to tell one story: the story of salvation history. We also believe that both are truly understandable only in light of each other. In other words, what is foreshadowed in the Old Testament is revealed in the New, and our understanding of what is revealed in the Old Testament is enriched by the Old.

When we look back through the pages of the Old Testament, we find all sorts of hints about what was to unfold in Israel's history, about the coming of the Christ, and about the establishment of a new type of kingdom. We also find hints about the woman who would give birth to the Christ and what her role in his kingdom would be. This is exactly why we're looking back through those pages for a deeper understanding of Mary.

We don't have to look far before we happen upon the first bit of Marian foreshadowing. It comes in the opening pages of Genesis,

the first book in the Bible. There, in Genesis 3, we find what biblical scholars call the *protoevangelium*, which is Greek for "the first
gospel" or "the first good news." This "good news" is God's promise
to Adam and Eve that, despite their sin, all hope is not lost for
man. There will be forgiveness and redemption. He foretells the
eventual downfall of Satan, telling the serpent, "I will put enmity
between you and the woman, and between your seed and her seed;
she shall bruise your head and you shall bruise her heel."[16]

The woman he refers to here is not Eve. She has already
sinned, and sinned gravely, so it is impossible for her to have enmity — that is, total and unmitigated opposition — toward evil.
And likewise it couldn't be one of Eve's natural sons who would
share in that enmity: that could be only Jesus himself. Based upon
that understanding of Genesis 3, there is, then, only one woman
to whom God can be referring in his words to the serpent: Mary,
the mother of Jesus.

In addition to that explicit Marian reference, there are two
prophecies in the Old Testament that foretell the Virgin Birth.
The first, in Isaiah 7:14, speaks of the "Virgin-Mother of Immanuel" and goes on to say, "Therefore, the Lord himself will give you
a sign. Behold, a virgin shall conceive and bear a son, and shall
call his name Immanuel." Later in Isaiah, Immanuel is referred to
as the future savior of his people, connecting the prophecy even
more clearly to Mary and Jesus.

Then, in Micah 5:2-3, the prophet foretells the birth of the
savior in Bethlehem from a woman who will "bring forth" the
"ruler of Israel":

But you, O Bethlehem Ephrathah, who are little to be
among the clans of Judah, from you shall come forth for
me one who is to be ruler in Israel, whose origin is from of

old, from ancient days. Therefore, he shall give them up until the time when she who is in travail has brought forth; then the rest of his brethren shall return to the people of Israel.

The mother, introduced so suddenly in Micah and so specifically designated without a husband, conveys the same virginal sense we see in Isaiah 7:14. The fact that she is so strongly and clearly identified as a woman without a husband represents at least an implicit reference to that same virgin birth.

In addition to these three explicit references to Mary as the mother of the redeemer, there are many other models, or "types," of Mary scattered throughout the Old Testament. Many of these models are the women of Israel: Eve, the first mother of the human race; Sarah, the wife of Abraham, who conceived miraculously in old age; Miriam, the sister of Moses, whose song, rejoicing in God's liberation of Israel, foreshadows Mary's song (called the *Magnificat*) of Luke 1:46-55; Hannah, who gave her son up to God's service; Bathsheba, the great Queen Mother of the Davidic Kingdom; and Esther, who interceded before her husband, the king, on behalf of her people, the Israelites.

There are also symbolic models of Mary, archetypal images that foreshadow the role she will play in salvation history. These include:

- *Jacob's Ladder*,[17] which was the intercessory means by which angels descended from heaven and ascended from earth in Jacob's dream.

- *The Burning Bush*,[18] which held within it the presence of God without material corruption.

- *The Israelites' Temple*,[19] the house in which God dwelt.

Perhaps the most important symbolic image of Mary in the Old Testament is the Ark of the Covenant.[20] It was built according to God's command, and his *shekinah*, or divine presence, hovered over it. The Israelites carried it with them through their desert wanderings, and when the great Temple of Solomon was built, it occupied the innermost sanctum, the Holy of Holies. What made the Ark so sacred, what actually made the inner sanctum the "Holy of Holies," was what was inside the Ark. Within its cedar walls lay the Ten Commandments, carved in stone, pieces of the Manna with which God had fed the Israelites in the desert, and the staff of Aaron, the first in the line of Levitical high priests. In other words, the Ark contained the Word of God, the Bread of God, and the most important symbol of a high priest of God.

When Mary was pregnant, what was it that she held inside her womb?

Jesus, "the Word of God made flesh."[21]

Jesus, "the Bread of Life."[22]

Jesus, the "eternal High Priest."[23]

Mary was a *living* Ark of the Covenant, home to the fullness of all that the first Ark contained and much more.

All of these images foreshadow in some way Mary's miraculous motherhood, her sorrows and sacrifices, her intimate relationship with her son, and her intercession on behalf of God's people. And all these Marian revelations were first seen in the infancy of Christianity, by the early Christian leaders and thinkers whom we call the Fathers of the Church

Mary in the Early Church[24]

The authors of the New Testament focus the overwhelming majority of their attention on Jesus and his ministry, not on his mother. The reasons for this are obvious: Jesus is God, Mary is not.

Meet Mary

If Christ's divine nature and primacy were not clearly and solidly established, devotion to his mother would make no sense; worse, it could morph into the type of goddess worship so common in the ancient Near East.

The same principle held true for the early Church. Establishing Christ's primacy had to come first; otherwise their claims to be the very Body of Christ would sound like lunacy. Yet even so, we still find acknowledgment of and devotion to the mother of Jesus from apostolic times.

The oldest historical evidence we have of Marian devotion among early Christians comes from the catacombs. These tombs of the Christian dead, scattered throughout the Mediterranean world, bear witness to their affection for Mary, their hope in her intercession, and their confidence in her place in heaven. As early as the end of the first century after Christ, they began including Mary in frescoes on the walls of the Roman catacombs. At times she is shown with her son; at other times she appears alone. Common images include Mary as the model of virginity and Mary as the *orans* — the woman at prayer. Scenes of Mary at the Annunciation and the Nativity are also on the walls.

One of the most significant frescoes is in the catacombs of St. Agnes in Rome. There, Mary stands between Peter and Paul, her arms outstretched to both. Dating back to the first years of Christianity, whenever Peter and Paul appear together in religious imagery, they are symbolizing the one Church of Christ, a Church of authority and of evangelization, a Church for both Jew and Gentile. Mary's prominent position between the two illustrates the Apostolic Church's understanding of her as "Mother of the Church."

The many images of Mary, and their location within the catacombs, also make it clear that the early Christians saw Mary not simply as a historical person, but as a source of protection and intercession. This symbolic use of her image points to the reality of their relationship with her. In seeing her as the Mother of the Church, they saw her relating to them, to all Christians, as any good mother would: protecting them, teaching them, and helping them by her prayers.

Then, within about a hundred years of Jesus' death, the leaders and teachers in the early Church had come to describe Mary as "the New Eve." What did they mean by this?

In Genesis, when Adam sinned, he did not sin alone. His wife disobeyed God before he did and then tempted him to disobedience as well. Man fell from grace, and Original Sin entered his nature because of Adam's sin, but Eve had played an instrumental role in that Fall.

So, too, with man's redemption. When man was given the possibility of being restored to grace and cleansed of Original Sin, that possibility came about through Christ's saving death on the Cross. But at the foot of that Cross was a woman, a woman who had made Jesus' death possible by making his life possible. With her yes to the angel Gabriel, Mary, like Eve, played an instrumental, albeit secondary role, in man's redemption.

St. Justin Martyr (d. 165), the early Church's first great defender of Christian teaching, made much use of this metaphor, describing Mary as the "obedient virgin" in contrast to Eve, "the disobedient virgin":

> [The son of God] became man through the Virgin [so] that the disobedience caused by the serpent might be destroyed in the same way in which it had originated. For Eve, while a virgin incorrupt, conceived the word that proceeded from the serpent, and brought forth disobedience and death. But

the Virgin Mary was filled with faith and joy when the angel Gabriel told her the glad tidings . . . And through her he was born . . .[25]

St. Irenaeus of Lyons (d. 202), another great defender of Christian orthodoxy, also wrote about Mary as the New Eve who participated in Christ's work of salvation:

Just as Eve, wife of Adam, yet still a virgin, became, by her disobedience, the cause of death for herself and the whole human race, so, too, Mary, espoused but yet a virgin, became, by her obedience, the cause of salvation for herself and the whole human race . . . And so it was that the knot of Eve's disobedience was loosed by Mary's obedience. For what the virgin Eve bound fast by her refusal to believe, this the Virgin Mary unbound by her belief.[26]

Later, St. Ambrose (d. 397) further developed the Christian understanding of the New Eve:

It was through a man and a woman that flesh was cast from Paradise; it was through a virgin that flesh was linked to God . . . Eve is called mother of the human race, but Mary was mother of salvation.[27]

St. Jerome (d. 420) neatly summarized the parallel when he wrote, "Death through Eve, life through Mary."[28]

In addition to this understanding of Mary's role in salvation history, the first centuries of Christianity also provide us with numerous examples of direct prayer to Mary as a means of intercession for the graces and protection of her son.[29]

St. Irenaeus referred to Mary as Eve's special "advocate," interceding through prayer for her foremother's forgiveness and salvation, while St. Gregory Thaumaturgus (d. 350) wrote of Mary in heaven praying for those still on Earth.

St. Ephraem (d. 373), one of the great Eastern preachers, prayed to Mary directly in several of his sermons, as did St. Gregory Nanzianzen (d. 389).

From the latter half of the fourth century on, such examples of Marian prayers simply abound, from the sermons of St. Ambrose to those of the Eastern Father St. Epiphanius. The most complete ancient prayer to Mary, however, dates back to an even earlier time, 250 AD. It is called the *Sub Tuum*:

> *We fly to your patronage,*
> *O holy Mother of God.*
> *Despise not our petitions*
> *in our necessities,*
> *but deliver us from all dangers,*
> *O ever glorious and blessed Virgin.*

The early Christians knew that the same woman who had rocked the infant Jesus to sleep, picked him up when he fell, and held his broken body in her arms could also be trusted to help them through their own trials, both spiritual and temporal. Their trust in and love for Mary was more than evident by 431 AD, when the Council of Ephesus — an authoritative meeting of Church leaders — formally defended her title as "Mother of God." Already, there were cathedrals dedicated to her in Rome, Jerusalem, and Constantinople, and after the council, devotion to Mary flourished even more in both the East and the West. Marian prayers, Marian liturgical feasts, Marian icons, and Marian paintings were soon everywhere in the Christian world.

The son's place had been secured, his Church established and fortified. And now, the seeds of truth about his mother, seeds

Meet Mary

foreshadowed in the Old Testament, planted in the New Testament, and cultivated in the early Church, could finally come to fruition. Nothing that came forth would or could in any way diminish the truth and glory of Christ. Rather, the fruits of authentic Marian devotion could only show more clearly, more beautifully, the possibilities offered to man by Christ's saving grace.

Chapter Two

She Kept These Things in Her Heart
The Four Marian Dogmas

The Bible and the writings of the Church Fathers have much to tell us about who Mary was and how the first Christians understood her role in salvation history. But does any of that matter to us, men and women who live in the twenty-first century?

As we'll soon see, it actually matters a great deal — perhaps more today than it has at any other time in history. First, however, we need to lay one more foundation, and that is an understanding of what the Catholic Church formally teaches about the mother of Jesus. These teachings, called dogmas, are the full flowering of the Marian "seeds" mentioned in the last chapter.

Dogmas Versus Doctrines

Catholics like to be very specific about words (such as *dogma*). The more specific we are in assigning meaning to a certain word, the less room there is for confusion and error. But some of our terminology, although we define it very carefully, can have different meanings in a secular context, or in Protestant denominations — thus, sometimes *leading to* confusion.

So, before I get into the four Marian dogmas of the Catholic Church, I thought it might be useful to explain how I'm using the word.

Meet Mary

A dogma is a teaching of the Catholic Church that has been formally defined — either by the Pope in a formal (called *ex cathedra,* or "from the chair") statement or by a Church-wide council of bishops held in union with the Pope — as true and binding for all believers. Besides formal definition, the other essential thing about dogmas is that they must originate, either explicitly or implicitly, in divine revelation: whether as found in the Bible or in the oral teachings given by Jesus and passed on through the Church since its beginning. In other words, the Pope can't just wake up one morning, declare that Jesus is from the planet Zebulon, and have that declaration suddenly become a new dogma of the Faith. It doesn't work that way. Dogmas are rooted in existing truths of revelation; the Church does not invent new ones.

Along with dogmas, there is also the broader category of *doctrines.* Now, all dogmas are doctrines, but not all doctrines are dogmas. How does that work? Simply put, dogmas are doctrines that have been formally defined. Doctrines are still official teachings of the Catholic Church, rooted in the Bible and Christian tradition, developed over the centuries by theologians, and talked about in sermons, prayers, and official Church documents, but they have *not* been formally defined by the Pope or by a council of bishops. Every single teaching on morality, for example, falls into this category: teachings such as the Church's prohibition of abortion, or its endorsement of charitable acts.

It's important to understand that doctrines are not second-rate teachings — somehow less important or less certain or less binding than dogmas. The faithful are to believe them just as much as dogmas. Historically, most dogmas were defined in order to defend a doctrine from a particular attack or misunderstanding, and many doctrines we have today have simply never been in need of such a defense.

The Four Marian Dogmas

So why am I boring you with all the dictionary stuff? Because it's especially important for our purposes that you understand the difference between *Marian* dogmas and doctrines. There are four Marian dogmas:

- Mary's status as Mother of God
- Her perpetual virginity
- Her Immaculate Conception
- Her Assumption into heaven

There are also Marian doctrines that have not been declared dogmas, but are still the authentic teaching of the Church, and which all Catholics, as Catholics, are supposed to believe. That distinction will become important in later chapters. For now, it's just important that you keep it in mind, as we move on to a closer examination of those four Marian dogmas.

As we will see, each truth about Mary both *protects* and *leads back to* the truths about Jesus. For example, her motherhood protects the truth that God the Son truly became a member of the human race. Her virginity helps us understand the fact that Jesus had no human father, but was conceived by the Holy Spirit. In life and in truth, Mary is the perfect mother who leads us without exception back to her Son.

Mother of God[30]

Not too long ago, I was talking with a Protestant woman who has a deep affection for Mary. "I really love Mary," she told me, "but it bothers me how you Catholics call her the Mother of God."

Puzzled, I asked her if she could explain what about that title troubled her.

"Well," she replied, "I don't like how it makes her seem greater than God."

Meet Mary

Although I admire the respect the woman has for motherhood — thinking that "mother of" means "greater than" — her understanding of this Marian title falls quite wide of the mark. If she were right, and that is what the title meant, then I, along with the rest of the Catholic Church, would err gravely every time we used it. But, most fortunately for us, it doesn't.

The title "Mother of God" arose from, and is best explained by, a simple syllogism: Mary is the mother of Jesus; Jesus is God; therefore, Mary is the Mother of God.

I can understand how a *non-Christian* would take issue with that syllogism. After all, if you don't believe Jesus is God, the bit about Mary can just be chucked out the window as well! The central and foundational belief of Christianity, however, is that the man Jesus of Nazareth was fully divine, the Second Person of the Trinity, one in nature with the Father and the Holy Spirit. Thus, if you deny that Mary is the "Mother of God," you're denying one of two things: either that Mary was really Jesus' mother, or that Jesus was really God. Since virtually no one bothers to deny that Mary did indeed give birth to Jesus, historical debate over the title "Mother of God" has quite logically revolved around the question of Jesus' divinity.

It was at the Council of Ephesus in 431 AD that the Catholic Church officially declared that Mary was the Mother of God, formalizing the long-believed doctrine as a dogma. This council, attended by Christian bishops from both East and West (and later confirmed by the Pope, the Bishop of Rome) had gathered in Ephesus for one main reason: to deal with a pesky priest named Nestorius.

Nestorius had taken it into his head that Jesus was not one person, but two — a human person and a divine person — and, at the time of the council, had been teaching this publicly. Accordingly,

Nestorius also refused to call Mary the Mother of God, since (he insisted) she was only the mother of Jesus the human person, not Jesus the divine person.

The council's response to Nestorius was to affirm as dogma that Mary is the Mother of God, the *Theotokos*, or "God-bearer." In doing so, it protected the truth revealed about Jesus in the Bible: that he is *one* divine person with *two* natures — a divine nature and a human nature — and that these two natures are inseparably united in the one and only divine person of Jesus. That is the truth that all Christians profess when we recite the Apostles' Creed: "We believe in Jesus Christ, his only Son, our Lord, who was conceived by the Holy Spirit, born of the Virgin Mary."

This truth not only protects what we believe about the divinity of Jesus, but it is also fully in keeping with the nature of motherhood. When a woman conceives a child, she gives to her child the same kind of nature she has: a human nature. But she doesn't merely give birth to a "nature" or even to a body. The fruit of the process of maternal generation is a *child*, a whole person. Your own mother is the mother of *you*, not just your body — even though you and I both know that she did not give you your soul, which was created and infused directly by God.

In that same sense, Mary is rightly called the Mother of God. She does not give Jesus his divine nature, nor does she give Jesus his divine personhood. Since he is God, both of those things have existed from all eternity. But neither did she merely "pass on" her flesh; she gave birth to the whole person of Jesus, in whom human nature and divine nature are inseparably united.

For that reason, we call Jesus both "Son of God" and "Son of Mary." And we rightly call Mary the "Mother of God."

So, in sum, when we call Mary the Mother of God, we are in no way declaring that she's equal to or greater than God, or that she existed before him (no merely human person can pre-date his mother, of course, but Jesus was not merely human!). We are simply affirming that she is the mother of Jesus, and more important, we are safeguarding the ancient belief that Jesus is one person, fully God and fully man.

Mary's Perpetual Virginity

Perpetual: that's the key word in the second Marian dogma, and that's also why Catholics and Protestants disagree on this teaching of the Catholic Church. Catholics believe that Mary was not only a virgin before and immediately after she conceived Jesus, but that her physical virginity remained intact during his birth, and in fact for the rest of her life. Many other Christian denominations hold instead that, after giving birth to Jesus, she and Joseph went on to have normal marital relations, and that she bore other children.

How on earth, they will ask, can a woman's physical virginity remain intact during childbirth? And what about those "brothers" of Christ mentioned in the Bible? Those are reasonable objections, and in a little bit, I'll offer what I think are some reasonable replies. For now, though, it would help to have a brief (actually, very brief) historical overview of this dogma.

Belief in Mary's perpetual virginity can be found in the earliest writings of the Church Fathers. In fact, across the board, from St. Ignatius of Antioch to St. Augustine, the belief is pervasive and unquestioned.[31] The teaching was finally officially defined in 649 AD, at the Lateran Synod, during the time of Pope Martin I. The entire council of bishops declared with the Bishop of Rome:

> The blessed-ever virginal and immaculate Mary conceived without seed, by the Holy Spirit, and without loss of integrity

brought him forth, and after his birth preserved her virginity inviolate.[32]

Let's take a closer look at those three phases.

• *Virginity before the birth of Jesus.* The witness of the Bible is clear on this point: Jesus had no human biological father. He was, in the words of the Apostles' Creed, "conceived by the Holy Spirit."

The prophecy in Isaiah 7:14 foretells Jesus' virginal conception: "Behold, a virgin shall conceive . . . a son." Likewise in the Gospel of Luke, we read that the angel Gabriel was sent by God "to a virgin . . . and the virgin's name was Mary."[33] When Gabriel tells Mary that she will conceive and bear a son, Mary responds, "How will this be since I have no husband?" — or, as translated literally — "since I know not man?"[34] *Know* here is to be understood in the biblical sense — in other words, as referring to sexual intercourse. Gabriel's response to her is, "The Holy Spirit will come upon you, and the power of the Most High will overshadow you."[35]

The early Church Fathers thus unanimously expressed their belief in Christ's virginal conception. Ignatius of Antioch (d. 107), Justin Martyr, and Irenaeus of Lyon (d. 202) are the earliest witnesses to this. To this day, Mary's virginity before the birth of Jesus is essentially a universally accepted truth among Christians.

• *Virginity during the birth of Jesus.* Disagreement among Christians arises, however, when we move to the question of Mary's virginity *during* the birth of Jesus. The Catholic Church teaches that Christ left Mary's womb without in any way causing her to lose her physical virginity; that her virginal seal remained intact. How is that possible? Well, although the early Church Fathers often compared the process to the way light passes through glass, the simplest answer is that it was possible in the same way that it was possible for her to become the mother of the Second Person of the Trinity: miraculously. Having given our belief to the one (greater) miracle, why should we stumble over the other (lesser) miracle?

Of course, Mary's authentic virginity means more than just a physical virginal seal: it refers to her complete self-donation, by which she gave her entire self, including her body, directly and exclusively to the Lord. But since human beings comprise both body and soul — since, as Pope John Paul II wrote, and as we will consider again later, *the body expresses the person* — it is appropriate that the woman who would go down in history as the perfect model of virginity consecrated to the Lord would have a perfect external, bodily virginity to go along with her internal, "moral" virginity.

Accordingly, the Church Fathers overwhelmingly taught that Jesus' "miraculous birth" resulted in no harm to Mary's physical virginity. St. Augustine stated, "It is not right that he who came to heal corruption should by his advent violate integrity."[36] And one of the early bishops of Rome, Leo the Great (d. 461), proclaimed, "Mary brought him forth, with her virginity untouched, as with her virginity untouched she conceived him."[37]

Later, Thomas Aquinas, the greatest biblical scholar and theologian of the medieval world, would defend the miraculous, and therefore painless, nature of Christ's birth. Since pain in childbearing was an effect of Original Sin, he said, the virgin mother, free from Original Sin (another dogma, which we'll examine later), would not experience pain during the delivery of the world's redeemer from sin.[38]

The Bible, too, bears witness to Jesus' virginal birth, although only implicitly. In Isaiah 7:14, the prophet says, "Behold a virgin shall conceive and bear a son." Note that he attributes both acts, conceiving and bearing, to a virgin.

• *Virginity after the birth of Jesus.* The third phase of Mary's virginity, her enduring virginity after the birth of Jesus, is also a point of disagreement between Catholics and Protestants. Non-Catholics typically point to biblical references to Jesus' brothers, or brethren.[39] Catholics aren't blind to these references, but with a full understanding of biblical language and context, and in the light of a tradition that so strongly supports her enduring virginity, we understand them differently.

The Greek word for *brother,* used in the biblical references to Jesus' brethren, is *adelphos.* Yet, throughout the Bible, the same word is often used to mean "cousin," or simply "close relative." There are, in fact, several instances where *adelphos* can't mean anything *but* close relative: for example, to describe the relationship between Lot and Abraham,[40] who were uncle and nephew, and between Jacob and Laban,[41] who were son-in-law and father-in-law.

Accordingly, because Catholics read the Bible with careful attention to their original languages, and within the context of the ancient traditions of the Church, when we see references to the *adelphoi,* or brothers, of Jesus in the New Testament, we understand that to mean his cousins, other relatives, or even possibly his close followers — *not* other children of Mary. Significantly, in the lists of his "brethren," none are ever called "sons of Mary." That phrase is reserved for Jesus alone.[42]

So, what do those ancient traditions have to say about Mary's virginity after the birth of Jesus? Quite a bit.

Mary's enduring virginity had a long list of defenders in the early Church. St. Ephraem, St. Ambrose, St. Augustine, St. Jerome, and many others all subscribed to the belief that Mary and Joseph never had other children or marital relations. It was explicitly taught by the Bishop of Rome as early as 392, and in 553, the Fifth General Council granted Mary the title "Perpetual Virgin."

An implicit scriptural reference to Mary's virginity after birth is also found in Mary's initial response to the angel Gabriel: "How will this be, since I know not man?" Many Church Fathers understood Mary's response to refer to a vow of perpetual virginity that she had already made and in which she had offered herself as a complete gift to God.[43] After all, since at the time of Gabriel's visit, Mary was already betrothed to Joseph, it would have been natural enough for her to assume that she would soon conceive and bear children. Her response only makes sense in the light of a vow of perpetual virginity. While there were others at the time of Jesus, such as the Essenes, who did take vows of celibacy, the perpetual vow of Mary is most appropriate in light of her perfect discipleship to Jesus. Like Son, like mother.

Why a Virgin?

Before moving on to the third Marian dogma, I want to make one thing clear: Catholics do not believe that Mary remained a virgin all her life because sex is a bad thing that would have somehow debased her. To the contrary, we believe, and the Catholic Church teaches, that sex is more than good, more than great; it is *holy:* a glorious gift from God that foreshadows the ecstatic union that we hope to enjoy one day in heaven with our God. Of course, like all gifts from God, sex can be abused, and its very holiness makes it all the more susceptible to abuse. Yet it only makes sense that the more precious something is, the more careful we have to be with it.

So, we don't have to place a high value on either virginity *or* sex, one at the expense of the other. We value them *both.* The witness of a godly marriage and the witness of consecrated virginity are both beautiful, both important, and both necessary. They are necessary because each speaks to a unique aspect of God and the relationship that he calls all of us to have with him. Indeed, our reasons for valuing virginity so highly are very similar to our reasons for valuing sex so highly. In heaven, while we will be enjoying the most intimate of interior unions with God, we will not be enjoying an intimate physical union with any of our fellow creatures. There will be no sex in heaven because there will be something better.

That means that those who make a vow of perpetual virginity in this life and who make it for the sake of the kingdom of God — priests, nuns, and consecrated religious, for example — are even more perfectly imaging the ecstasy in the world to come. They are giving everything of themselves, including their gift of sexuality, to God here and now, as a sacrifice. And only good and valuable things make acceptable sacrifices.

All of this, however, still raises the question, "Why?" For what purpose did God allow Mary to remain a virgin in the act of giving birth, and why did Mary choose to remain a virgin for the remainder of her earthly life?

Catholics find an answer to that question (and I think a very good answer) in the way we understand the relationship of the body and the soul.

Every human being is a union of body and soul, not simply a soul that inhabits a body, like a hermit crab in a shell. If we tumble down the stairs, we don't say, "My body fell down and my soul went along for the ride"; we say, "I fell down." The Catholic Church further teaches that when God created man, he made both the body and the soul good. So perfect was the harmony between them that, in all its actions, the body expressed the soul — made the soul *visible* with complete accuracy. When man fell from grace, however, he lost that harmony, and sin infected both the body and the soul. After that, the body would continue to express the soul, but only imperfectly, and the soul and body would no longer cooperate in harmony.

In light of this understanding, we can see why Mary's physical virginity is so important. For the Christian faithful, she embodies what it means to give oneself entirely to the Lord, to live with restored obedience and integrity. Her yes to the angel Gabriel, the selfless motherly love she gave to Jesus in their home in Nazareth, and her acceptance of his sacrifice on the Cross were all acts of surrender to the divine will. Maintaining her virginity was another exterior sign of that interior gift of herself.

In addition to that defining reason, over the years some of the Catholic Church's greatest preachers and scholars have seen additional reasons why virginity was fitting, although not strictly necessary, for Jesus' mother.

Thomas Aquinas explained that, as the only-begotten Son of the Father, Jesus possessed an unfathomable dignity, such that, when he became man, likewise demanded that he be the only-begotten son of his human mother. Aquinas also pointed out that Mary's womb was, quite literally, a *shrine* infused by the Holy Spirit and dwelt in by the Son. It would not be fitting for that same sacred place to be used to gestate and issue forth ordinary sinful men and women.[44]

In our modern world, which has lost a great deal of respect for the sacred, this idea can seem a bit overdone. But perhaps we would do well to recapture the sense of awe and reverence for holy things that generations before us possessed. I can think of no better place to begin than with the womb in which God himself dwelt.

The Immaculate Conception

The Immaculate Conception is not the Virgin Birth.

I want to make that really clear at the beginning of this section, since far too many people, including some Catholics, get hopelessly confused on that point. *The Immaculate Conception is not the Virgin Birth*. Furthermore, the conception that was "immaculate" was *Mary's*, not Christ's.

The dogma of the Immaculate Conception says that at the very moment of Mary's conception, both her soul and her body were created without the stain of Original Sin; they were *immaculate*. The dogma of the Immaculate Conception does *not* say that Jesus' conception was "immaculate" because it didn't involve sex (all of us who were conceived in the ordinary way are not "stained" thereby, because, if you remember, sex is a good thing created by God).

Now that we have that out of the way, let's look more closely at this dogma. When Catholics talk about Original Sin, we're referring to the inherited wound all men and women have in their souls. That wound was inflicted by the sin of our first parents (Adam and Eve), has been passed on from parent to child since that Fall, and will continue to be passed on until the end of time.[45] The effects of the wound are known all too well. We don't even have to look around at all of the evil and hatred in the world to see them. All we have to do is look inside ourselves — at our own tendencies to selfishness, our own jealousy, our own anger — to know what Original Sin has done to human nature and to know that it's not a pretty sight.

Although referring to the "stain" of Original Sin is a pretty common metaphor (I used it myself a couple of paragraphs back), it's not quite accurate. Original Sin isn't something that was added to the human soul, the way a stain mars clean clothing. It's more like something that was *taken away*, something now lacking in the soul: namely, the grace that God originally intended us to have within us. That grace was to be the spiritual sustenance for our earthly life, our heavenly life, and for our relationship with God in both lives. When Adam sinned, however, that grace was lost, and man no longer had enough sustenance to live as he was supposed to live.

Catholics believe that when Christ died on the Cross, he made it possible for men and women once more to have access to spiritual life, to the grace we so desperately need. We also believe that we receive that heavenly help when we profess our faith in Christ and are born into new life through Baptism, and, by that help, we can have our souls healed, growing in grace and sanctity in this life until we are fully transformed by it in the next.

But thanks to her Immaculate Conception, Mary never suffered the deprivation of grace to begin with. She was full up from the start. That fullness of grace enabled her to choose the good and the right every day of her life. Like our first parents, who also were created with a certain fullness of grace, she could have sinned. But she didn't. Not once. In any way.

Now, Mary's sinless nature was not something she earned on her own or even merited. It was a grace, and like all grace, it was a pure gift from God. And even though it occurred in time prior to her son's redemption of the world on the Cross, that grace flowed from the Cross all the same. God, because he's God and outside of time and can do things like that, applied the merits Jesus earned on Calvary to Mary at the first instant of her existence. That means Mary owes her salvation to God as much as any of us — or rather, more so, since she was redeemed from more: not only saved from sin but completely untouched by it.

The seeds of this teaching are found in both the Old and the New Testaments. In Genesis 3:15, after Adam and Eve have lost the fullness of grace, God addresses Satan, represented by the serpent, and says, "I will put enmity between you and the woman and between your seed and her seed; she will crush your head, and you shall lie in wait for her heel."[46] As we said earlier, *Jesus* is the seed that is victorious over the evil seed of Satan. That means the woman God refers to is Mary, the mother of Jesus — not Eve, the mother of a grand bunch of sinners.

Importantly, the word *enmity* does not mean mere "dislike" or "mild distaste for," but rather "complete and total opposition." (Other places where the Hebrew word for *enmity* is used in the Old Testament refer to scenes of violent opposition, and even to struggles unto death.) Now, in theory, I am in complete and total opposition to sin. I think it's a very bad thing, and I try not to do it. *Try* is the operative word there, for as much as I dislike it, I still sin. This means that I'm really not in a state of complete and total opposition to sin. Enmity does not exist, in the truest and fullest sense of the word, between Satan and me.

Now, had Mary sinned in any way at any point, she, too, would have been in at least partial participation with Satan. But that would directly contradict what God tells us in Genesis 3:15.

In the New Testament, we also see the origins of this teaching when Gabriel appears to Mary.[47] When he greets her, he says, "Hail, full of grace." Not, "Hail Mary," but "Hail, *full of grace*." "Full of grace" is what he calls her. He refers to her by it as by a name. The Greek term for "full of grace" is *kecharitomene*, a big word with a complex meaning even for those who know biblical Greek, for it refers to a sanctifying action *that was accomplished in the past-perfect tense*. That's why the angel's greeting can be best translated, "Hail, you who have been perfected in grace."

Remember, perfection in grace is just what the rest of us are lacking. Those of us who have accepted Christ and received the gift of baptism receive great graces, as well as the capacity to re-ceive more graces, but we know through simple experience that we're not perfected in grace. But Mary did have the fullness of grace: she is what God originally intended all of us to be. And the angel's greeting to her tells us that she had been granted that full-ness at some point in the past: at, we believe most logically, the very instant of her conception.[48]

As with the other Marian dogmas, we find ample evidence in the teachings of the Church Fathers that Mary's fullness of grace and her freedom from sin have been taught from the earliest days of Christianity. They refer to Mary under such titles as "all holy," "all pure," "most innocent," "a miracle of grace," "purer than the angels," and "altogether without sin." And that was just within the first three centuries after Christ.

The early Church Fathers also compared Mary's sinless state to Eve's sinless state before her fall. Mary, as the "New Eve," was be-lieved to have enjoyed the same state of original grace and justice that Eve was granted in the Garden. Since Eve was obviously cre-ated in a state of grace, without the fallen nature the rest of us have inherited from her and Adam, the parallel made between Eve and Mary by the Church Fathers likewise illustrates their un-derstanding of Mary's immaculate creation.

In the words of St. Ephraem, "Those two innocent . . . women, Mary and Eve, had been [created] utterly equal, but afterward one became the cause of our death, the other the cause of our life."[49]

St. Ephraem also alluded to Mary's sinless nature when, ad-dressing Jesus, he wrote, "You and your mother are the only ones who are immune from all stain; for there is no spot in Thee, O Lord, not any taint in your mother."

As time went on, references to Mary's Immaculate Conception became more and more explicit and developed. St. Ambrose of

Milan (d. 397) referred to Mary as "free from all stain of sin." St. Severus, Bishop of Antioch (d. 538) stated that Mary "formed part of the human race, and was of the same essence as we, although she was pure from all taint and immaculate." St. Sophronius, Patriarch of Jerusalem (d. 638) signaled that Mary's purification indeed occurred from the first moment of her existence when he wrote, "You [Mary] have found the grace which no one has received . . . No one has been pre-purified except for you."[50]

Such testimonies (and there are many others) from the early Church Fathers are particularly important, because they lay to rest another common misconception about the dogma of the Immaculate Conception: namely, that Pope Pius IX made it up, pulled it out of thin air, when he proclaimed it an official Catholic dogma in 1854. As we saw earlier, before being officially proclaimed by the Church, dogmas have to be solidly rooted in the ancient teaching of Jesus and the Church. That's what gives them authority.

In the end, though, it really shouldn't be all that hard to believe in Mary's Immaculate Conception. After all, God originally intended for *all* of us to be immaculately conceived. His first plan was that every man and every woman would begin their life in the family of God. Only because of the Fall are we now conceived without that fullness of grace. Mary is for us the shining exception, but she ought to have been the norm.

Nonetheless, her preservation from sin was a singular privilege. This free gift from God to Mary prepared her to be the perfect mother of God made man. And it was supremely appropriate (although not absolutely necessary), that Mary should pass on to Jesus, the spotless lamb without sin, a human nature identical to her own, just as our mothers passed on to us natures identical to their own. The difference being, of course, that Mary's nature should also be, and was, immaculate.

Think of the opposite possibility. Imagine that God the Son had to come into direct contact with Original Sin in becoming man because his mother, in her body and soul, was contaminated with the victory of Satan, his chief adversary. Did God not empty himself enough by taking on our limited human natures without having to have his flesh given to him by one directly wounded by his ancient foe?

No, it was *right* that the one who came to redeem humanity from sin should receive his own human body from a woman who benefitted chiefly and preemptively from his eventual victory over sin. It was *fitting* that Jesus should receive his immaculate body, the very instrument of human redemption, from a mother who had been given the fullness of grace.

The Assumption

The dogma of the Assumption declares that at the conclusion of her earthly life, Mary's body was preserved from all physical corruption and *assumed*, along with her soul, into heaven. The doctrine of the Assumption was made a dogma in 1950 through an *ex cathedra* statement by Pope Pius XII, but the teaching itself, as with all dogmas, goes back to the Bible and the traditions of the early Church.

The first hint of Mary's Assumption comes once more from Genesis 3:15. There we see the mother of the redeemer, sharing in her son's victory over evil: "I will put enmity between you and the woman and between your seed and her seed . . ." What does that have to do with the Assumption, you ask?

Well, if you flip ahead in your Bible, you'll see that in Romans 5-8 and Hebrews 2, St. Paul tells us that the effects of evil, of Satan's seed, are twofold: sin first, the corruption of death second. Mary's sharing in her son's victory over evil, therefore, means that she would, like her son, be free from all stain of sin and escape the fate of bodily corruption after death. By preserving her from sin at conception, God gave Mary the amazing privilege of being born with a fullness of grace. And in the Assumption, the fitting book-end to the Immaculate Conception, her body was spared from the ravages of corruption.

More biblical support for the teaching comes from Luke 1:28, since Mary's bodily Assumption would be a natural effect of be-ing "full of grace"; and furthermore, from Revelation 12:1, where Mary appears in heaven, crowned with the sun. Importantly, Mary's appearance comes immediately after St. John tells us that the Ark of the Covenant has appeared in the heavens; remember that the Ark was one of the first Christians' most common meta-phors for Mary, who, just as the Ark had done, carried the pres-ence of God within her.

It shouldn't surprise you by now to hear that the early Church believed in this dogma. In the early fourth century, not long after Christianity became legal in the Roman Empire and it became possible to build public places of worship, the Christians in Rome built a grand church in Mary's honor. Today, that church is known as the Basilica of St. Mary Major. In that church, constructed in approximately 360 AD, is a historical testimony to the early belief in Mary's Assumption: a fresco depicting the mother of Jesus being lifted up to heaven by the angels.

In the sixth century, St. Gregory of Tours wrote, "The Lord com-manded the holy body [of Mary] to be borne on a cloud to paradise, where, reunited to its soul and exalting with the elect, it enjoys the everlasting bliss of eternity."[51] From the seventh century onward, numerous Church Fathers, including St. Germain of Constanti-nople (d. 733), St. Andrew of Crete (d. 740), and St. John Dama-scene (d. 749) wrote and preached about the Assumption.

During the sixth century, the first liturgical feasts dedicated to the Assumption appeared in Syria and Egypt. Western liturgical feasts celebrating the Assumption began taking place in Gaul (modern-day France) in the seventh century, and by the eighth century, it was celebrated in Rome. From the thirteenth century on, the doctrine of Mary's Assumption was being universally celebrated throughout the Church in both the East and the West.

When Pius XII declared Mary's Assumption an official dogma of the Church, he pointed out that there are essential connections between the Assumption and the other Marian dogmas, particularly the Motherhood of God and the Immaculate Conception.[52]

We've noted how Mary's Assumption is the logical effect of her being preserved from Original Sin. Adam and Eve would likewise have been assumed, uncorrupted, at the end of their earthly lives. Mary, the new Eve, enjoyed what the first Eve lost through sin.

Pope Pius also remarked how appropriate it was that Jesus chose to honor his mother as only a divine son could. Jesus perfectly fulfilled the Jewish Law, including the Ten Commandments. Included in those commandments, number four on the list, is "Honor thy father and mother." Because perfectly fulfilling the law meant perfectly honoring his mother, it makes sense that Jesus would uniquely honor his mother, first, by preserving her from the corruption of the grave and second, by granting her glorification of the body in heaven before the general resurrection of the body for all other saints on the last day. After all, who among us, if it were in our power, would do less for our own mothers?

Another question that often arises in connection with the Assumption is this: Did Mary die? Well, the Church has never definitively said one way or the other. The majority of Catholic and Eastern Orthodox theologians, however, do think it likely that at the end of her earthly life, Mary did die, and by *die*, we mean a

temporary separation of the soul and body, in which the body suf-
fers no manner of bodily decay. Her death, however, must have occurred in circumstances beyond our ordinary human experience.
Mary did not die as most of us do, from disease or from mortal ag-
ing. This would not be possible in light of her Immaculate Conception, which safeguarded her from the punishments revealed in
Genesis due to sin, including death and decay.

Her body would not experience decay, before or after death,
because bodily corruption was an effect of the Fall, and Mary's Immaculate Conception would prevent her from the punishment of
bodily breakdown. Her death is, like her Assumption, fitting, because, as the model of the perfect disciple, she would have wished
to imitate her Son in all things, including death.

∞

How beautifully and appropriately does the life and truth of the
mother radiate the splendor and the glory of the son! Her divine
motherhood enfleshes our redeemer as a God who loved us so
much that he truly becomes one of us to save us. Her virginity reveals his divine and heavenly origins and exemplifies Mary's perfect discipleship to Jesus. Her Immaculate Conception is the
greatest fruit of his glorious Redemption and brings our savior into
the world in complete separation from the evil one. And her Assumption foreshadows the ending victory of each person who accepts Jesus as Lord, in word or in charity.

These four central dogmas of Jesus' mother — her divine motherhood, her perpetual virginity, her Immaculate Conception, and
her Assumption — reveal the unique role Mary of Nazareth played
in God's plan of salvation. However, they also point to how Mary
continues to play an important role in the life of the Church and
of all believers.

Chapter Three

Behold, Your Mother
Mary's Spiritual Motherhood

When we meet new people who interest us, we spend time getting to know them. We talk about their past, their favorite books, their political beliefs, and all the other bits and pieces of their lives that make them who they are. The point of all that talking is not just to accumulate facts; rather, we're seeking to build a relationship with them. We want to *know* them, not merely know about them.

What is true in the natural order is also true in the supernatural order. We've spent so much time going over the facts about Mary — who she is, where she comes from, and what her friends say about her — not to study her from a distance, but to build a *relationship* with her. In fact, the Catholic Church teaches that whether or not we know it or like it, all Christians are already in a relationship with Mary. She is, in the order of grace, the mother of all believers. She is our mother.

No, of course she didn't give birth to us, rock us to sleep, or wipe our noses when we were little. But we do believe that, by the grace of God, Mary has been given the special task of being a spiritual mother to mankind. The Bible tells us so quite directly, in the Gospel of John. From the Cross, Christ looks down upon Mary and the Beloved Disciple (St. John referred to himself that way deliberately, to make himself representative of every Christian), who are standing at its foot. To Mary he declares, "Behold, your son," and then to the Beloved Disciple, "Behold, your mother."[53] Jesus' words do not come in the form of a request or an invitation. They are a command, a statement of the way things are going to be.[54]

Thus, in Revelation 12 — where, if you recall, Mary is depicted as a woman clothed in the sun and wearing a crown of twelve stars — St. John refers to her "other offspring, those who keep God's commandments and bear witness to Jesus." In other words, the Bible says that all those who follow Christ are automatically Mary's children. The very nature of discipleship demands it. That's why the Beloved Disciple immediately took his new mother "to his own home."[55]

The Meaning of Motherhood

So what exactly does Mary's spiritual motherhood entail? Until about forty or fifty years ago, I could have answered that question simply by saying, "Everything that natural motherhood entails, but on a supernatural level." Unfortunately, that answer no longer works so well, because our culture no longer shares a clear idea of what natural motherhood is all about. Motherhood has come under attack in our day; been ridiculed, rejected, and endlessly redefined. So, in order to understand how Mary can be a supernatural mother to mankind, we first need to reconstruct our understanding of natural motherhood.

Men and women are different (regardless of what some people would like us to believe!). And some of those differences are made clear to us in an immediate and visible way through our bodies. After all, the body is the visible expression of the soul. It gives exterior form to the interior person. And the particular form that a woman's body takes expresses, among other things, her interior disposition to motherhood. It also gives us clues as to the essence of motherhood itself.

The whole constitution of a woman's body — her womb, her breasts, even her skin, which is softer than a man's and thus more comfortable for infants' own tender skin — reveals her innate orientation toward giving and nurturing life. As soon as a new life is conceived within her, the woman's body becomes a home for the unborn child, providing him with protection, nourishment, and warmth. During pregnancy, the mother's voice, the rhythm of her heartbeat, and the pressure of her hands grow familiar to the child and, eventually, help awaken the unborn baby's consciousness.

After birth, the mother's body remains wholly oriented toward the care of her newborn. Her breasts swell, filled with milk that provides the baby with all the nutrition he needs, as well as antibodies to fight illness and hormones to increase his contentment.

Even in these first simple bodily acts, mothering transcends simply nourishing the baby's body. The child's constant nearness to the mother while she holds and nurses him helps him develop the patterns of speech necessary for learning language. Touch, the only one of the five senses common to the whole of the body, makes the mother concretely present to the infant. In turn, that increases his awareness and hope for love and care.

Throughout her child's early years, the essential acts of motherhood first revealed by the body — nourishment, nurturing, education, and sacrifice — continue to define her relationship with the growing child. With her hands, she still cares for the child's body, feeding, cleaning, and clothing him. And with her arms, eyes, and mouth, she still communicates her presence and love. But as the child grows, her mothering becomes more and more focused on the child's interior development, and she becomes responsible for mediating the world to him.

Through the mother, a child learns to know his father and siblings. Through her, he learns to speak, read, and eventually write his first words. Through her, he encounters men, women, and other children, and learns by example how to live in relationship with them. As she delights in and encourages her child in his accomplishments, she helps him to develop his God-given gifts to their highest potential.

Most important, through her teaching and example, her child comes to know himself as a child of God and learns what it means to follow Jesus. He learns to love by returning her free and selfless love.

Mary performed all those acts of mothering — nourishing, nurturing, praying, educating, and sacrificing — for her son, Jesus, during his earthly life. From her body, he received his humanity, and in her arms he encountered his first loving gaze. She carried him in her womb, bore him with her body, nursed him at her breast, cleansed him with her hands, and kissed him with her lips. In an awesome reversal that defies human understanding, Mary was God's "first tutor in love."

And at Calvary, when Christ commanded the beloved disciple to behold his mother, he announced that everything Mary had done for him in a natural way, she would, from that moment on, do for all believers in a supernatural way.

In other words, as our mother in the order of grace, Mary helps give us new life in Christ, sustains that life through her prayers, and teaches us what it means to live a life rooted in faith, hope, and charity.[56]

Giving Life

Natural motherhood begins with giving birth to new life. Mary's spiritual motherhood likewise begins with her participation in giving spiritual life to human souls. Our very ability to *have* a spiritual life — a life lived in communion with God both here and in eternity — depends on two things: that God became flesh and that God gave up his flesh. If you don't have the Nativity, you don't have Calvary, and if you don't have Calvary, you don't have the Redemption.

So, the Incarnation and the Cross. One takes place in Nazareth, the other in Jerusalem, and thirty-three years elapse between the two events. But the same two people are present for both: Jesus and Mary.

Now, Jesus' presence is a given. After all, the whole work of redemption depended primarily on him. But, it didn't depend *exclusively* on him. God himself chose to have some of the responsibility rest on a young girl from Galilee, a young girl who didn't have to accept the responsibility, a young girl who could have said no when the angel came calling. But she didn't. And with her yes at the Annunciation, Mary began her journey toward supernatural motherhood, conceiving within her not only the life of the God-Man, but also the possibility of supernatural life for all men.

Mary's yes continued to Calvary, where she remained by her son's side until his final hour. There, she accepted his command to become the mother of all his disciples, and there she gave her final acceptance to the Father's will for her son. Through all these acts of obedient acceptance, she participated in the work of the world's redemption. Because of this, you will sometimes hear Catholics refer to Mary as the "Co-redemptrix." This does not mean that she was Christ's equal in the work of our salvation. It simply means she played a real and substantial part in her son's work. By God's design, Mary's yes both at the Annunciation and on Calvary mattered in a uniquely important way. St. Paul called on every

Christian to be a "fellow worker with God,"[57] and Mary did just that, in a way no other creature ever had or ever will.

Mary's cooperation in her son's work would also bring upon her a share of her son's suffering. The Bible attests to this reality from the first pages of Genesis. There, God foretells of the enmity he will place between Satan and the mother of the Redeemer. Again, here enmity means total and complete opposition to evil. And while being in complete opposition to evil is always a good thing, it isn't always an easy thing. In a fallen world, there's often a cost for doing good, and since Mary did good every day of her life, she would have paid that cost again and again.

Other biblical passages bear witness to Mary's sufferings. Remember that after Jesus' birth, the prophet Simeon warned her that a sword would pierce her heart.[58] The book of Revelation depicts the mother of the male child "who is to rule all the nations" "cry[ing] out in her pangs of birth, in anguish for her delivery."[59] Mary did not suffer in giving physical birth to Jesus; but she did suffer in giving spiritual birth to us, with Jesus, on Calvary.

The early Fathers of the Church also saw Mary's participation in the work of Christ as the beginning of her supernatural motherhood. Characterizing the Incarnation as "the Redemption anticipated and begun," Sts. Irenaeus and Epiphanius spoke of Mary as "the cause of salvation" and "the mother of the living," while St. Jerome proclaimed simply, "Death through Eve, life through Mary."[60]

Mary's participation in the Redemption was unique. But (and this is a big *but*) her participation was completely subordinate to and dependent on her Son's. Once more, that favorite analogy of the Fathers — Mary as the New Eve — holds true here. Just as Eve gave the fruit to Adam as the instrument for the fall of humanity, Mary gave Jesus his flesh to be the instrument for the redemption of humanity. Through her yes at the Incarnation and her sufferings on Calvary, she helped give life to new souls, to our souls. But the ability to do that was hers not by right, but rather by gift. The same thing could never be said of Jesus Christ, who is the author of our life and our salvation.

Nourishing Life

A mother can give life to her child, but if she does not actively care for him afterward — feeding him, educating him, providing for all his needs — most of us wouldn't think her much of a mother. That's why, if Mary can truly be called our spiritual mother, she has to have some part in nurturing and nourishing our souls.

On the most basic level, she fulfills this motherly obligation by modeling for us what it means to be a true disciple of Christ. With no thought for herself, Mary accepted God's will for her life and became the mother of the Messiah. She took no pride in God's choosing her or in how he graced her. She rejoiced in those gifts, but she always knew they were gifts, for which God deserved all the credit. The words of her *Magnificat* — her song of rejoicing in Luke 1 — express this beautifully:

> *My soul magnifies the Lord,*
> *and my spirit rejoices in God my savior,*
> *for he has regarded the low estate of his handmaiden.*
> *For behold, henceforth all generations will call me blessed;*
> *for he who is mighty has done great things for me,*
> *and holy is his name . . .*

Not only does Mary teach us obedience and humility; she also teaches us attentiveness to God's word. The Gospel of Luke tells us twice that "Mary kept these things [the details of Jesus' life and words], pondering them in her heart."[61] Her eyes were always on her son, and everything he did, everything he said found a place in her soul.

Mary also exemplifies for us the ideal of Christian service. When she herself was pregnant with none other than God made man, she traveled far from home to care for her cousin Elizabeth. As my wife or any other woman who has borne children can tell you, traveling when you're pregnant is no picnic. And that's traveling in modern speed and comfort. For Mary, traveling into the hill country where Elizabeth lived most likely meant a combination of walking and riding on the back of a donkey. Lots of fun. Yet, just as she gave of herself to bring God into the world, Mary gave of herself to help others in need, regardless of what it cost her. She was a selfless servant.

Perhaps what Mary teaches us best, however, is how to suffer. Because Mary never sinned, no selfishness, ego, or vanity ever dimmed her love for her son. She loved him perfectly. And because her son was God, he was the perfect object of love. That means that at Calvary, perfect love endured the torture and death of perfect love. That endurance was obedient and accepting. It saw, in the midst of all the pain, a more perfect and more loving will at work, and it united itself to that will. That is how Mary suffered, and that is how God calls us all to bear our sufferings.

Mary, however, does more than just model discipleship for us. For no mother loves merely by her example. Mothers love through their actions.

That is exactly why the Catholic Church believes that Jesus allows his mother to give us the graces we need to grow in faith and why we honor her with the title of "Mediatrix of all graces." We do not honor her with that title because she is the author or source of those graces, but because she brought Christ, the source of all grace, into the world; and because, by his grace, she still acts as a channel for bringing all the graces of redemption into the world. The graces are his. They originate in him. But he puts those resources at her disposal and allows her to give them to each of us according to our individual needs. So, when we are fighting temptation, she gives us the gift of strength. When we endure the loss of a loved one, patience in suffering comes to us through her. When persecutions come our way, she sustains us with forbearance. All of the gifts come from Christ, but, so that Mary might fulfill all the obligations of a true mother, God allows them to come to us through her.

As the Bible shows us, the Incarnation initiates this mediation of Mary in time, when she brings forth Christ, the source of all grace, into the world. When Mary visits Elizabeth, she literally brings grace into her home by bringing the unborn Jesus in her womb. The unborn John the Baptist recognizes this physical mediation of grace by leaping in his mother's womb when he encounters Mary and her unborn child. Mary later presents her child to the shepherds and the Magi who come seeking him.

The early Church Fathers taught that this mediation of grace, begun in time, continues in eternity. St. Cyril called Mary the one "through whom the tempter, the Devil, is cast down from heaven, through whom the fallen creature is raised up." St. Germain of Constantinople wrote of Mary, "No one secured a gift of mercy save through you." St. Ephraem went so far as to say, "After the Mediator, you [Mary] are the Mediatrix of the whole world."[62]

∞

Okay, I keep throwing around this word *mediation* (and *Mediatrix*), and I know that word can be a bone of contention between Catholics and Protestants. After all, St. Paul clearly states that "there is one mediator between God and men, the man Christ Jesus."[63] So, how do I reconcile that with the Catholic understanding of Mary's maternal mediation?

First, let's define *mediator*. In general, a mediator is a person who intervenes between two parties with the goal of reconciling and uniting them. As Christians, we believe that there is only one unique mediator who reconciles man with God, and that is Jesus Christ. But the perfect mediation of Christ doesn't prevent other mediators who are subordinate and secondary to Jesus. In fact, it *provides* for them.

We see several examples of this kind of secondary mediation in the Old Testament. We have the prophets, who work to bring the people back to Yahweh and Yahweh to the people. We also have the patriarchs, men such as Abraham and Moses, whom God used to form a covenant with his chosen people, and whom he also used to bring about the fulfillment of his promises to those same chosen people. In both the Old and New Testaments, the glorious mediation of the angels fills the pages, as they bring messages and gifts from the Lord to his people. They bear messages to Abraham, Mary, and Joseph. They also do battle in the Lord's name against the powers of darkness, battles witnessed by the prophet Elijah and the apostle John.

Such forms of mediation are not only permissible, but they're prescribed in Scripture. In fact St. Paul's very words in 1 Timothy 2:5 about there being "one mediator between God and men" are immediately preceded by the following:

First of all, then, I urge that supplications, prayers, and thanksgivings be made for all men, for kings and all who are in high positions, that we may lead a quiet and peaceable life, godly and respectful in every way. This is good, and it is acceptable in the sight of God our Savior, who desires all men to be saved and to come to the knowledge of truth.[64]

So, from the context of 1 Timothy 2:5, we can see that Christ's mediation does not exclude the secondary mediation of others, since "supplications, prayers, and thanksgivings" made on behalf of others are clearly examples of mediation. And, in our own lives, we see this at work all the time. Every time we offer up a prayer for someone to receive the gift of healing, of hope, of faith, of love, we are acting as *mediators* between that person and God. The same goes for every sacrifice of praise and every fast. All of those acts demonstrate our participation as secondary mediators in the one mediation of Christ — without which none of our prayers or sacrifices would do any good.

If you and I, sinful and weak as we are, can participate in Christ's mediation and be a source of grace and strength for those we love, why should it surprise us that Christ's mother participates in his perfect mediation to an even greater degree? Mary was born to give Christ to the world. During her time on earth, she lived to give Christ to the world. And now, in heaven, she still lives to give Christ to the world. And, in the end, that is exactly what all those gifts of grace do: they give Christ to us, and they enable us to give ourselves, ever more truly and wholly, to Christ. Mary's ability to bring that about is a privilege of the highest order, and it is a privilege from which we can all benefit eternally.

Sustaining Life

What human mother doesn't pray for her child? Even if she has no faith at all, when she sees her child suffering, when she fears for his safety, she'll offer up a prayer in desperation to a God she only hopes exists. And what mother, when her child comes to her with a real need, doesn't want to do everything in her power to see that need met?

Mary does no less for us. The Catholic Church teaches that she is our constant advocate before God. She allows none of our pleas to go unheard. More important, like all mothers with little children, she knows our needs better than we do and presents our petitions to her son more effectively and more truly than we ever could.

She also knows how hard life can be for us here on earth. She knows how we struggle with temptation, and she knows that most of us are just one breath away from giving in to them. Because of that, she is always before her son, obtaining for us the grace we need to overcome those struggles, to choose what is good and right, and to live a life of obedience, love, and faith. This role has earned her the title of "Advocate" in the Catholic Church.[65]

Mary's role as a maternal Advocate is foreshadowed in the Old Testament, where one of the key elements of the Davidic kingdom was the role of the Queen Mother, or *Gebirah*. Beginning with Bathsheba, Solomon's mother, the *Gebirah* was the people's chief intercessor before the king. Mary, shown in Revelation 12 as the queen of heaven, wearing a crown of twelve stars, is also recognized as such by her cousin Elizabeth in Luke 1:43. When Mary enters her cousin's house, Elizabeth calls her "the mother of my Lord," an ancient title used to refer to the *Gebirah*. At Cana, Mary takes the needs of a family to her son, obtaining for them the miraculous grace of fine wine.[66] Revelation 12 also speaks of how she does battle with the Devil, who wages war against her children on earth.

Christians have turned to Mary as a maternal advocate since the earliest days. As we talked about earlier, there remain a number of images of Mary on the walls of the catacombs and the actual

tombs of the first Christians, invoking her protection and intercession. Believers offered prayers to her, asking for spiritual and
physical protection. Witness, for example, the *Sub Tuum*, which
dates back to 250 AD: "We fly to your patronage, O holy Mother
of God. Despise not our petitions in our necessities, but deliver us
from all dangers, O ever glorious and blessed Virgin."

Remember, only by her son's grace do Mary's prayers have such
efficacy. But efficacy they do have. It is just one of the many ways
he has chosen to honor the woman who loved and served him for
so many years in their home in Nazareth. Before Jesus laid down
his life for all of us, Mary laid down her life for him, giving everything to the son she loved and the God she adored. Now, in eternity, he returns that honor by letting her love, just as powerfully
and just as effectively, all of us, her children on earth.

Living Communion

All Christians share a common historical statement of belief:
the Apostles' Creed. Prayed by believers for at least the past 1800
years, the creed expresses the basic tenets of the Christian faith.
One tenet that comes near the end of that prayer professes the
Christian belief in "the Communion of Saints." What that means
is that we believe Christians are all part of the one Body of Christ;
that, regardless of when or where we live, we are united in a living
relationship with every other man, woman, and child who professes — or did or ever will profess — faith in Christ. That relationship allows us to pray for one another, strengthen one another,
and comfort one another as we journey through this life and into
the next.

Our relationship with Mary is one of the most beautiful and
powerful examples of that communion. Mary is a woman who
knows what it is to suffer, who knows what it is to sacrifice, who

knows what it is to love. She gazed upon the face of Jesus from his infancy until his death, and she made a total offering of herself and her life to him. There's no one in the history of the world who knew him better. And through God's providential and perfect design, he now allows us to be in a relationship with this woman — to turn to her in our times of need for motherly intercession, to look upon her as an example of what it means to love God with our whole hearts, our whole minds, and our whole strength, to seek comfort in the very arms that comforted our Lord.

In no way does this diminish God's own glory, or our need for his grace. Our need for him is unchanging and everlasting, and our relationship with him should always be the primary one in our life. Yet it is for the sake of that relationship, and at his express invitation, that we are also called into a relationship with the woman who brought him into this world. That is a divine privilege that blesses us and glorifies God. If we neglect that privilege, we are ignoring Christ's solemn command and refusing one of his greatest gifts.

Chapter Four

All Generations Shall Call Me Blessed
Marian Devotion

All relationships, of course, are a two-way street. They require something from us — phone calls and visits, acts of thoughtfulness, time spent together. They demand that we give something of ourselves to the other. In our relationship with Mary, she helps give new life to our souls, prays for us, and provides us with what we need to grow in grace. In return, she deserves our honor and love, just as our earthly mothers do. She deserves our devotion.

To make sure we're all on the same page, I want to spend a little time explaining what I mean by *devotion*. The word can have more than one meaning, and the Church uses Latin terms to help us distinguish between the kind of devotion we give to Mary and the kind of devotion we give only to God. These words are *dulia* and *latria*.

Latria basically means adoration. Traditionally, it refers to the worship and homage that we give to God and God alone. When we adore God, we acknowledge him as an excellent, perfect, uncreated, divine person. We give him what he alone, as God, is due.

Dulia is very different. Essentially, *dulia* means love and honor; that is, praising the excellence of a created person. We see this particular kind of honoring every day, when, for example, people are recognized for their achievements in sports, academics, and the arts. But we never think that honoring a baseball player goes against or takes away from the adoration we give to God.

Now, Catholics believe that we should not only honor those who excel in the things of this world, but that we should also honor those who excel in the things of the spiritual world (for example, in their devotion to God, their obedience to his will, and their charity to others). That's why we honor the saints — men and women who, during their earthly life, excelled in their pursuit of holiness. Honoring the saints does not detract from God any more than honoring athletes does. In fact, when we honor saints, we are honoring God, too, for it is by his gifts, and for his glory, that saints are able to excel in holiness in the first place. When we praise those who spent their life pursuing an intimate union with God, we ultimately praise God, who is both the giver and the object of that love.

Now, if it's fitting to venerate those who have achieved spiritual excellence, isn't it even more fitting to venerate the woman who achieved it to the highest degree: the woman whom Jesus chose to become his mother in the order of nature and our mother in the order of grace? Of course it is. And in recognition of Mary's pre-eminent holiness, the special recognition we give to Mary is called *hyperdulia*: the greatest amount of honor we can give to any created person.[67]

Again, this special veneration of Mary is completely different from, and inferior to, the adoration we give to God. We adore God and only God, and since Mary is not God, we don't adore her. It's as simple as that. Don't get confused if you happen to see the expression "worship of Mary" in an old Catholic book. The English language is flexible, and the word *worship* in many of those old books can mean either *hyperdulia* or *latria*. In reference to Mary, though, it never means the kind of adoration due to God alone.

The Catholic Church, in fact, strictly and expressly prohibits the adoration of Mary as divine. Still, because of who Mary is, what she did during her earthly life, and what she continues to do in eternal life, she is more deserving of veneration than any other created creature — man or angel — that ever will exist. That's why the term *hyperdulia* is used to describe only the type of honor we give to Mary.

Higher than the Angels

Let's go into a little more detail on why Mary merits her own unique level of veneration.

As the Catholic Church understands it, there are three fundamental reasons Mary deserves a higher level of devotion than all other holy men, women, and angels.

The first reason is that God chose to give Mary a *fullness* of grace. From the first moment of her conception, Mary possessed the fullness of grace — the fullness of life — that God originally intended all men and women to possess. Free from Original Sin, she passed on her own immaculate human nature to her son, Jesus. This can't be said of any other created person. All of the other saints the Church honors, and all of the men and women whose holiness only God knows, received a great deal of grace in their lifetimes, certainly, but they never received the fullness of grace. They were all born with fallen natures, and only a nature free from all stain of sin can possess that fullness. Mary alone was given that privilege. Her possession of such a singular gift makes her deserving of a singular type of devotion.

Second, and more significant, Mary alone had the privilege of being the mother of God, of Jesus Christ. She was the one who gave flesh to the "Word made Flesh." She was the one who carried him in her womb and watched him day by day as he grew "in wisdom and in stature and in favor with God and man."[68] Because she was ever in his presence, Mary's relationship with Jesus was entirely different from the relationship that any other person has ever had with him. Only Mary had an interior and essential role in Jesus' taking on flesh and becoming our redeemer. Only Mary had a physically and spiritually intrinsic role in the Incarnation.[69] All other men and women, even St. Joseph, no matter how closely associated with the Incarnation, had only an external relationship with God becoming man for the sake of our salvation. This uniqueness cannot be underestimated. To underestimate the role of Mary in God's becoming man is, in fact, to underestimate the significance of God's becoming man.

The third reason Catholics believe Mary deserves a greater degree of veneration than all other creatures is her obedience. The words Mary uttered at the Annunciation, she also uttered with her heart every day of her life. "Let it be to me according to your word" was not just a one-time deal with Mary. She lived all of her years on earth in perfect obedience to the Father. His will was her will. Sustained by his grace, Mary perfectly modeled a life of virtue. She still models that for all believers. She shows us what it means to surrender ourselves and receive everything as a gift from God. She shows us the path to true freedom, true happiness, true life. And for that, too, she deserves a devotion like no other.

Because God gave Mary such an important role in the story of our salvation, devotion to Mary should not be an arbitrary or extraordinary thing. It should just be a normal part of the faith life of all believers.

This, of course, leads us to the question: What does devotion to Mary look like? How do we hold up our end of the relationship?

How do we respond in a fitting way to this woman, to this mother, who does so much and gives so much to us?

Probably the best way to answer that question is to look at some of the most common forms of devotion Catholics have practiced through the centuries. They are truly simple acts and have been performed by the most humble of men and the littlest of children. At the same time, some of the greatest intellects the world has ever seen have also found in them, not simply love, comfort, and understanding, but the beginning of true wisdom and the keys to unlocking some of the greatest mysteries of the Christian faith.

The Rosary

Of all the acts of devotion that Catholics give to Mary, the Rosary is probably the most common, the most beloved, and the most important. No other prayer has been prayed by so many people in so many countries and across so many centuries. And no other prayer has done so much for so many hearts. During his first few weeks as pope, in 1978, John Paul II described the Rosary as "my favorite prayer, a marvelous prayer." He then went on to explain why:

> Against the background of the words, *Ave Maria* [Hail Mary], there passes before the eyes of the soul the main episodes of the life of Jesus Christ, and they put us in living communication with Jesus through, we could say, his mother's heart. At the same time, our heart can enclose in these decades of the Rosary all the facets that make up the life of the individual, the family, the nation, the Church, and all mankind, particularly of those who are dear to us. Thus, the simple prayer of the Rosary beats the rhythm of human life.[70]

So, what is this prayer that draws us into "living communica-tion with Jesus" through "his mother's heart"? Essentially, it's a combination of vocal prayer and meditation upon the central mysteries of Christ's life. It is an *incarnational* prayer in that it gives both the body and the soul a part to play. The basic structure of the prayer consists in praying twenty sets (referred to as "decades") of ten Hail Marys, with an Our Father prayed at the beginning of each decade (see the appendix for a closer look at how to pray the Rosary). While we pray each decade, we meditate on one of the central mysteries of Christ's life. In doing so, we imitate Mary her-self, who, Scripture tells us, interiorly "made her own" the sacred events in the life of her son: "Mary kept all these things, pondering them in her heart."[71]

Technically, to pray one "Rosary" means to say the full twenty decades, with one Gospel mystery associated with each decade. The twenty mysteries, however, are categorized into four sets of five mysteries, and typically most Catholics don't pray all four sets of mysteries in one sitting. Most pray one set a day, and change which set they pray, depending on the day of the week. These sets are:

- *The Joyful Mysteries*, which center on the events of the In-carnation: the Annunciation,[72] the Visitation of Mary to Elizabeth [Visitation of Elizabeth by Mary?],[73] the Birth of Jesus,[74] the Presentation of Jesus in the Temple,[75] and the Finding of the Child Jesus in the Temple.[76]

- *The Luminous Mysteries*, which center on the key events of Christ's earthly ministry: his baptism in the Jordan,[77] the Wedding at Cana, where Jesus performed his first public miracle,[78] the Proclamation of the Kingdom of God,[79] the Transfiguration on Mount Tabor,[80] and the Institution of the Eucharist at the Last Supper.[81]

• *The Sorrowful Mysteries*, which focus on the Redemption by Jesus' Passion and death: the Agony in the Garden,[82] the Scourging at the Pillar,[83] the Crowning with Thorns,[84] Jesus' Carrying of the Cross,[85] and the Crucifixion of Jesus.[86]

• *The Glorious Mysteries*, which center on the mystery of eternal life: the Resurrection of Jesus,[87] the Ascension of Jesus into Heaven,[88] the Descent of the Holy Spirit at Pentecost,[89] the Assumption of Mary into Heaven,[90] and the Crowning of Mary as Queen of Heaven.[91]

History of the Rosary

The Rosary has been around in one form or another since the early thirteenth century. Traditionally, Catholics trace the origin of the prayer back to St. Dominic Guzman (d. 1221), who traveled through southern France preaching against the Albigensian heresy. The Albigensians denied the infinite goodness and power of God and taught that all matter was evil. They also attacked Christian morality and opposed the doctrines of Creation, the Incarnation, the Redemption, and eternal life. In the midst of combating this heresy, St. Dominic is said to have begun preaching on the mysteries of salvation and, at the end of each instruction, reciting ten Hail Marys, allowing prayer to do what his preaching could not. According to this tradition, the Virgin Mary herself inspired St. Dominic to adopt this unique form of preaching.

After this beginning, the structure of the Rosary went through a period of gradual development. The Catholic laity (those not ordained as priests or consecrated as monks or religious sisters) recited 150 Hail Marys in imitation of the 150 psalms prayed daily by the monks. They incorporated the use of beads to make it easier to count the prayers, and added fifteen Our Fathers to break up the

150 Hail Marys into sets of ten. This prayer form, based on the Our Father and the Hail Mary, became known as Our Lady's Psalter.

The specific Rosary mysteries also went through a great deal of development. In the fourteenth and fifteenth centuries, Catholics meditated upon fifty to a hundred mysteries during the recitation of the 150 Hail Marys. Gradually, the Church reduced the number of mysteries to fifteen, and in 1569, Pope Pius V approved what would be the basic form of the Rosary for the next 433 years, until, in 2002, Pope John Paul II introduced a new set of mysteries — the Luminous — to the existing Joyful, Sorrowful, and Glorious Mysteries.[92]

Although the basic form of the Rosary has remained virtually unchanged for the past 500 years, Catholics of different times and places have always found ways to make it uniquely their own. To-day, in several countries, including the United States, France, and parts of Germany, the Rosary begins with the Apostles' Creed, an Our Father, three Hail Marys (often prayed for an increase in faith, hope, and charity) and a Glory Be. In many Spanish-speaking countries, however, the Rosary ends with that series of prayers, while, in other countries, those prayers are sometimes not said at all. Catholics have added and subtracted other prayers over the years, and individual men and women in their private prayer lives have chosen additional mysteries and events from the Bible to meditate upon. Ultimately, this diversity reflects the nature of the Rosary itself — a deeply personal meditation on the events of Christ's life, death, and Resurrection and how those events apply to our own journey to eternal life.

Christian Meditation and the Rosary

Perhaps, before I go any further, I should take a minute to elab-orate on what I mean by *meditation*. In our culture today, we hear a lot about different forms of meditation. Oprah Winfrey and Hollywood starlets are always going on and on about the importance of meditation in their lives, and various forms of Eastern meditation are all the rage in health clubs and yoga centers from New York to San Francisco. That kind of meditation — rooted in the traditions of the Orient and focused mainly on the self — is not what happens in the Rosary. When we finger our beads and say our Hail Marys, Catholics are practicing an entirely different type of meditation. We're practicing Christian meditation.

In its most basic form, Christian meditation is the prayerful focusing of the mind and heart upon some supernatural truth or object. It typically involves three basic elements: consideration, application, and resolution.

• *Consideration* is when the mind intellectually but prayerfully considers the spiritual subject in question. One example of this would be reflecting on Christ's carrying his Cross to Calvary.

• *Application* follows contemplation and consists of applying the truths of the spiritual subject to our own life. Application means answering questions such as, "What does the way Christ carried his Cross have to do with me and my own spiritual life?" or "How do I respond to the crosses and trials that come my way — in a Christlike way?"

• *Resolution* is when we make some practical resolve in our own spiritual lives based on the truth and application of the mystery. It is, for example, to say, "I resolve with the help of God to bear my sufferings more patiently and more humbly, giving thanks that I am allowed to suffer as Christ suffered for me."

That, in sum, is Christian meditation, and that is the type of meditating we do when we pray the Rosary. Those interior reflections are the inner life of the Rosary, the soul of the prayer. Meditating on the mysteries brings an interior attention and devotion to the words said aloud, transforming what would otherwise be simply a string of repetitious phrases into an intimate encounter with God — into prayer.

The Heart of the Rosary

So, why the Rosary? Why is this one prayer so treasured by Catholics and such a loving act of devotion to the mother of Jesus? There are many answers to that question, probably as many as there are people who pray the Rosary. But for the sake of brevity, let's talk about what I think are three of the most important reasons.

First, the Rosary is biblical. It is, in a way, a compendium of the entire Gospel.[93] The twenty mysteries of the Rosary walk the believer through the New Testament, telling the tale of Christ's life, ministry, death, and Resurrection. They also point to the destiny Christ offers to each of us — namely, eternal glory.

Beyond the biblical nature of the Mysteries, the prayers themselves are biblical. The Our Father is the prayer Christ gave to his disciples when they came to him, saying, "Teach us to pray."[94] And the Hail Mary is also, fundamentally, a scriptural prayer, joining together the greeting of the angel Gabriel to the mother of Jesus in Luke 1, "Hail, full of grace, the Lord is with you" and the greeting of Elizabeth to Mary later in that same chapter, "Blessed are you among women, and blessed is the fruit of your womb." That second part of the prayer expresses the same sentiments found in the *Sub Tuum*, the first recorded prayer to Jesus' mother, and asks for her prayers for her children on earth, "Holy Mary,

Mother of God, pray for us sinners, now and at the hour of our death."

By reciting the words of the New Testament and contemplating the truths revealed therein, we come to a deeper understanding of the mystery of our redemption. We grow in knowledge about the faith, and we grow in love for Jesus. Because that type of growth is what every loving mother wants for her biological children, Mary could want nothing less for her spiritual children.

The second reason for the Rosary's pre-eminence is that the prayer is Christocentric: Jesus himself is the focus of the entire prayer. His life is at the heart of the Gospel mysteries, and his word is the origin of the prayers. Eighteen of the twenty mysteries focus on moments from his life on earth. The last two mysteries — the Assumption and Coronation of Mary — illustrate how Christ applied to his mother the graces he merited on the Cross. And, in a way, both of those last two mysteries point to the way all believers will benefit from those graces. Mary's Assumption foreshadows the resurrection of the body, which all of the faithful will experience on the last day. Mary's Coronation is a sign of the crown of glory that St. Paul tells us Christ promised to those disciples who successfully run the race of life. Both mysteries are a foretaste of all that Christ's followers hope for in the life to come.

The prayers of the Rosary are also centered on Christ. The words of the Our Father are Christ's own words, given to his disciples long ago. The words of the Hail Mary are the words of Gabriel and Elizabeth, words spoken to her because of her relationship with Christ. The two parts of the prayer are joined by the name of Jesus. His name is at its heart.

As I said in the introductory chapter, what Mary desires, what Mary considers her task as our spiritual mother, is to draw all her children closer to her first child, Jesus. Devotion to Mary never

ends with Mary. Its proper end is always Christ. The Christocentric nature of the Rosary accomplishes that in a very con-
crete way.

Finally, the Rosary's importance comes from the way it reflects
and elevates our human nature. As human beings, we are by nature a union of body and spirit. And when Christ came into the
world, he took on flesh, also becoming a union of body and spirit.
In order to be truly and fully human, neither can be jettisoned.
Both are, in the most accurate sense of the word, essential. Accordingly, when we worship God, we are called to worship him
with our whole being, both body and soul. Kneeling, folding our
hands in prayer, and raising our arms in praise are all ways we do
that. So is praying the Rosary.

By joining together vocal prayer and meditation, the Rosary
becomes incarnational prayer. It demands something of both
the head and the heart, of the body and the soul. Our fingers'
passing over the beads frees our souls from the practical distrac-
tion of counting and enables us to focus on the prayers and
Mysteries. The fingering of the beads[95] and the forming of the
words also draws the body into prayer, focusing it and keeping it at
the disposition of the soul. In a way, meditation is the "soul" of the
Rosary, while the vocal prayer and the fingering of the beads is its
"body."

The Rosary's ability to embody prayer in a physical act is a reflection of Christ's Incarnation and of the essential union existing
between our own body and soul. By its very nature, it draws us into
these two truths and helps us live out who we are in relation to
God just as we typically live out who we are in relation to the
world.

The Rosary is not about endless or mindless repetition. The
Rosary is about salvation history. It is about Christ and about

humanity. Through praying the Rosary, we grow in intimacy with Christ's mother and ultimately with Christ himself. And that is exactly why the prayer has held such a place of honor in the prayer lives of countless holy men and women for the past millennium, and why praying it regularly is one of the greatest little acts of love we can give to Mary.

∞

There are two other important Marian devotions that have had an elevated place in the lives of Catholics through the centuries: the Brown Scapular devotion and Marian Consecration. Like the Rosary, they are little acts that convey our great love for her as Christ's mother and our own.

The Brown Scapular

The word *scapular* comes from the Latin *scapula*, which means "shoulder." The Brown Scapular consists of two small pieces of cloth connected by strings and is worn over the shoulders as a symbol of the protection and love of Mary. According to Catholic tradition, the devotion was given by Mary herself to St. Simon Stock, a thirteenth-century Carmelite priest. Appearing to him in a vision, she held out the scapular to him and said, "This will be for you and for all Carmelites the privilege, that he who dies in this will not suffer eternal fire."

Essentially, the wearing of the Brown Scapular offers the promise to all who faithfully wear it that, in the end, their souls will be saved through Mary's intercession. I know, I know: to a lot of people that sounds as if Catholics who wear the scapular are banking on something other than Christ for their salvation, or think they can earn salvation through some act of their own. But that's not it at all.

First, a person can't wear the scapular, go around breaking God's law left and right, and still get a free pass into heaven. The scapular is not a magical charm. Faithfully wearing the scapular means that there has to be an *interior disposition of fidelity* to Christ. The scapular then becomes the exterior sign of that fidelity, as well as a sign of trust in Mary's love for all her children and of her ability to intercede for us before her son. In some ways, it's like a wedding ring, which serves as an exterior sign of a wife's fidelity to her husband or a husband's fidelity to his wife.

Unlike the wedding ring, however, the scapular is more than just a sign. It's an efficacious sign. That means that, to a degree, it can be an actual vehicle for the grace that helps the person cultivate and maintain that fidelity. Catholics believe that just as grace came into the world through matter — the matter of the human body of Jesus Christ — so does grace continue to come to each of us through matter. For example, it comes to us through the waters of Baptism, through the bread and wine that becomes Holy Communion, and through hands graced with the power to heal bodies and spirits. To a lesser degree, therefore, it can also come to us through the reverent wearing of a couple of pieces of brown cloth joined with some string and worn in love as a symbol beyond itself.[96]

Grace, of course, ultimately comes from only one place, from one person, and that is Christ himself. He is author of the grace that comes into this world; and it is his free gift. Mary's prayers for us and our donning a scapular that possesses the means to be an instrument of grace in no way diminishes either of those fundamental truths. Wearing the scapular is simply another way of disposing ourselves to receive that grace. It is our response to his offer through her. It is the putting out of our hands for what Christ seeks to give us through her.

Marian Consecration

Another centuries-old devotion to Mary is Marian Consecration, a promise of love and a gift of self that gives all that the person is and does completely to Jesus through Mary. In other words, Marian Consecration means giving yourself entirely to Mary so that she can exercise even greater maternal care over your soul and body in order to help you conform ever more closely to Christ's image. Traditionally, the Church Fathers referred to this as making ourselves the servants of Mary, and the practice itself is based on Mary's ability, granted to her by Christ, to dispense the graces he merited on Calvary to all his followers.[97]

As with other forms of Marian devotion, Marian consecration is, ultimately, about Christ. As the great eighteenth-century saint Louis de Montfort put it, we "do all our actions through Mary, with Mary, in Mary, and for Mary, so that we may do them all the more perfectly through Jesus, with Jesus, in Jesus, and for Jesus."[98] Marian consecration should never be seen as a gift of love that stops solely with Mary, but a consecration of self that will always end in the heart of Christ. It is not an end, but a means — a means that recognizes Mary as the physical instrument through which Christ came into the world and which also recognizes her spiritual capacity to be the means by which all men and women can come to know and love Christ.

Today there are two common forms of Marian consecration: the form promoted by St. Louis de Montfort (see appendix) and the form promoted by the twentieth-century saint and martyr Maximilian Kolbe. Both require periods of intensive reflection and prayer, and those periods themselves become a means through which we draw closer to Christ.

There are also shorter forms, and it is not uncommon for a person to consecrate himself each morning to Mary with the knowledge that everything we give to her will in turn be given to Christ.

Marian consecration is the most supreme act of love we can give to the mother of Christ. Supreme not only because it honors her for her obedience, her humility, and her gift of self to God, but supreme because in giving ourselves to her, we enable her to lead us ever more deeply into a loving relationship with her son. And that is what she desires above all else.

What about Those Statues?

I'm about to wrap up this chapter, but before I do, I want to say a few words about "those statues." You know, the statues of Mary that fill Catholic churches, sit in our gardens, and have a place of honor in our homes. The ones you often see Catholics kneeling in front of and might cause some to think, "Hmmm . . . idol worshiper?"

We've already dealt with the worship part of that equation (recap: Catholics don't worship Mary as a deity), so let's talk about the idol part. By definition, an idol is something we set up as a god and adore. The golden calf in the book of Exodus is a famous example. When the Israelites were none too happy with Moses' disappearance for forty days and nights, they decided to forsake the God of their fathers and worship a golden idol, as the Egyptians did. That, of course, was a very bad idea, and the Israelites spent many a year afterward regretting that little indiscretion. That was also a very different sort of thing from what Catholics do when we kneel before a statue of Jesus' mother.

First, you would be hard-pressed to find a Catholic kneeling before a statue of Mary who actually thought he was kneeling before a god (or a goddess, as the case may be). We're quite aware that statues are inanimate objects — pieces of plaster, wood, or stone, not gods. Secondly, those statues weren't made for the purpose of giving Catholics an image of an "alternate god" before whom they could bow down. There is one God, and it's not Mary.

Rather, the statues were made for the same reason we print pictures of our earthly loved ones: like the photograph of your mom that you frame and put on the mantel. The statues are simply a representation, a reminder of a person we're called to love and be in a relationship with. When we look at the statues or kneel down out of respect and veneration, they make her more present to us, more real, just as looking at a photograph of a loved one makes them more present and more real. It's an act of devotion, not idol worship.

Let's not forget that God didn't save us from up in heaven. He came down, took on a human nature, died on a Cross, saved us in *this* world. That's called the *incarnational principle* of salvation. It should serve as little surprise, then, that Jesus would use the signs and symbols, materials and images of this world to help us remember and live the life of Christian faith he calls us to imitate. From holy water to blessed objects to statues of Mary, holy "things" remind us of our humble Jesus, who became "matter" himself to help us sanctify our own lives in this material world.

∞

The Rosary, the Scapular, Consecration, and even kneeling before a statue are all, in the end, small gifts of love that have helped countless men and women grow in love for the mother of Jesus. They are what we give back to her for all she gives to us. Through the centuries, they have helped Christians understand Mary's joys and Mary's sorrows in this life and helped them to imitate her unwavering obedience and devotion to her son. They have, through her eyes, glimpsed the miracle of the Incarnation and the power of the Redemption. They have unlocked a treasure house of grace and, most important, they have drawn those who practice them into a more intimate, more loving union with Jesus himself. And that is what Marian devotion is really all about: loving the son, by loving the mother.

Chapter Five

Clothed with the Sun
Mary in Private Revelation

Imagine that you have a son who is away at college and is behaving, unfortunately, like some young men do when they're out of Mom and Dad's house for the first time. (I know, for some of you, this doesn't take a whole lot of imagining.) He's out late partying, blowing off his classes, and not behaving in the most gentlemanly of manners. And he makes no attempt to hide this from you. He seems to have no shame. So, what do you do?

First you e-mail him. You drop him a casual line or two saying, "You know better. Shape up." That doesn't have quite the effect you were hoping for, so you pick up the phone. You have a little conversation and remind him *why* he knows better. But again, nothing changes. In fact, the situation is getting worse. He's in danger of failing out. Do you send him another e-mail or make another phone call? No. You get in the car and drive to his dorm to have a little chat. The situation had become so urgent that only a personal visit could get your message across.

In essence, this is what private revelations or apparitions from Mary, or the saints, or God himself, are all about: urgent personal visits to have a little chat with us wayward sons.

Of course, a lot of people, even Catholics, are doubtful about private revelation in general and about Marian apparitions in

particular. Such caution is not a bad thing. Genuine private revelations are exceedingly rare, and false ones can pose a spiritual
danger to the overly credulous. So it's healthy to be initially skeptical about people's claims to have seen, heard, or spoken with a
heavenly messenger.

However, being skeptical is different from being *completely
closed to the possibility* that God can and does continue to speak to
his children in the world, both directly and through his messengers. To out-and-out deny that possibility is, in effect, to deny either God's omnipotence or his love. But if you accept that God
has the power to appear to his creatures or to send a messenger
from heaven to appear to his creatures, and if you accept that God
so loves his wayward children that he'll do everything he can to
get their spiritual houses in order, then accepting the possibility of
apparitions should not be that much of a stretch.

Accordingly, on the basis of those first two assumptions, the
Catholic Church has, over the centuries, accepted as credible certain claims of apparitions from Mary or other messengers from
God. So, as Catholics, we believe not only that Marian apparitions are possible; we believe that they have indeed happened. If
we are to develop our relationship with Mary to its fullest potential, it is fitting to examine some of those events and see what we
can learn from them. But before we address the whys, whats, and
wheres of Mary in private revelation, we should first gain a firm
understanding of private revelation itself.

Theology of Private Revelation[99]

The first and most important thing to know is that private revelation is *not what we read in the Bible*. Scripture, along with its development and interpretation in tradition is *public* revelation. The
term *revelation* itself comes from the Latin word *revelare*, meaning

"to unveil or disclose." So, public revelation is God's disclosing of divine truths to humanity for the sake of our salvation. All Christians believe that God transmits these truths to us through the Bible. Catholics would add that Sacred Tradition is another vehicle for public revelation. But, all Christians agree that public revelation ended with the death of the apostle John.[100]

Private revelation, on the other hand, is when God gives a specific message to an individual or group — or even the entire Church — for their spiritual benefit. Unlike public revelation, private revelation does not communicate new doctrines of the Faith, necessary for salvation. God revealed everything we needed to know about him and our place in salvation history to the people of Israel who wrote the Old Testament and to the Apostles and early followers of Christ who wrote the New Testament.

Yet, although there is no need for further public revelation, there is a great need for Christians of all stripes to be regularly reminded of what it means to be a follower of Christ. The ordinary means for delivering such reminders include the preaching and pastoral guidance of our ministers, the liturgical life of the Church, spiritual reading, and fellowship with other Christians. But sometimes God chooses to deliver a reminder through the extraordinary means of private revelation: giving the faithful special words of wisdom, encouragement, and correction to help us live the Christian life more fully.[101] Private revelation is all about God's calling us back to gospel truths, especially the harder truths that demand from us prayer, fasting, penance, conversion, and sacrifice.

Theologically, private revelation is associated with the gift of prophecy mentioned throughout the letters of Paul.[102] In the New Testament, when God granted someone the gift of prophecy, he made him the bearer of a special revelation that would encourage other believers. That gift was made possible by an outpouring of the Holy Spirit and was foretold by the prophet Joel: "And it shall come to pass afterward, that I will pour out my Spirit on all flesh; your sons and your daughters shall prophesy, your old men shall dream dreams, and your young men shall see visions."[103] The Acts of the Apostles names some of the early Christians who were granted this gift, including Agabus and the four daughters of Philip.[104]

After the last books of the New Testament were written, private revelation continued in the early Church. Accounts of this are recorded in the *Didache* (a collection of Christian teachings from the late first century/early second century) and in the second-century account of the Shepherd of Hermas. Through the centuries, the Church continued to recognize authentic private revelation, believing that the faithful would always need these extraordinary calls to return to the life of grace. As St. Thomas Aquinas wrote in the thirteenth century, "At all times, there have not been lacking persons having the spirit of prophecy, not indeed for the declaration of any new doctrine of faith, but for the direction of human acts."

The Forms of Private Revelation

Private revelation usually is given to a person through a vision, a locution, or a combination of both. When it comes through a vision, it typically takes one of three forms.

The first form is a *corporeal* vision. This is where a divine messenger physically appears — or at least seems to appear — before the "visionary." That is to say, the visionary sees God's messenger with his eyes. This happened to numerous people throughout the Bible, including Mary herself, when the angel Gabriel appeared before her. Today, corporeal visions are what you will typically hear referred to as "apparitions."

Other types of visions include *imaginative* visions — which are perceived not by the senses, but rather, by the imagination, either while the visionary is awake or asleep — and *intellectual* visions, which are directly perceived by the mind, again while the visionary is awake or asleep. Some visions can exhibit several of these characteristics at the same time.

Another vehicle for private revelation is a locution. Locutions are supernatural messages that can be received corporally, intellectually, or by the imagination. Sometimes locutions accompany visions, and sometimes they don't. Both visions and locutions, however, can come directly from God, from Mary, or from a saint or an angel.[105]

The Church and Marian Apparitions

Because of the possibility of human deception (or of demonic influence), the Catholic Church exercises extreme caution and diligence before it declares a reported Marian apparition to be authentic. It makes rare declarations only after a long period of careful observation and investigation. (That the last two centuries have witnessed more Church-approved Marian apparitions than any other time in history, then, says a great deal about the state of the world and God's current level of concern for it.) The Church conducts its investigation, and bases its conclusion, on a set of criteria that can be divided into three categories:

• The content of the revealed message;

• The nature of ecstasy and other concurring phenomena;

• The spiritual fruits.

First, the Church examines any message revealed through private revelation in the light of Christian teaching and tradition. If the reported message in any substantial way contradicts the Bible or the Church's doctrine, the "revelation" must be false. This is because the Holy Spirit, who is the source of both public and private revelation, cannot contradict himself. He doesn't reveal one truth at one point, and then reveal a completely contradictory truth at another. We humans contradict ourselves and change our minds all the time. God does not. His truth and his word are unchanging.

This does not mean that there cannot be minor errors in the reports of authentic private revelation. As long as God delivers messages to fallible human beings, there will always be the possibility for small mistakes when the visionary attempts to communicate the message to others. But the message itself must always be in complete harmony with public revelation and Christian doctrine.

Second, the Church carefully studies the supernatural phenomena accompanying the reported revelation, particularly the ecstasy experienced by its recipient. *Ecstasy*, put simply, is a physical manifestation of a spiritual state, in which the visionary is partially removed from an ordinary space-and-time experience and brought partially into the temporal spatial experience of the messenger of the revelation. In that state, the visionary's body does not respond to physical stimuli in the way it ordinarily would.

In medieval times, Church examiners would sometimes test whether a person was actually experiencing ecstasy by sticking a needle into his arm! Today, the Church relies on the much-improved modern means of medical-scientific testing, including EKG, EEG, and other technologies, to distinguish genuine ecstasy from a false report.[106]

Other supernatural phenomena that can figure into the Church's investigation include material signs or events that can't be explained by natural means, but only by a direct intervention of God. In the past, these signs have included a solar miracle (at Fatima) and a miraculous spring (at Lourdes).

Finally, the third major piece of criteria the Church uses to evaluate a reported apparition is the spiritual fruits that come from it. After all, "the tree is known by its fruit."[107] One of the best indications that a revelation is authentic is when it actually produces the type of conversion of hearts and souls that is always the ultimate end of all true private revelation. This type of conversion is typically visible for all to see and includes a return to or increase in prayer, worship, and the practice of Christian virtue.

The Church must be shrewd in evaluating apparent fruits. It's possible for false apparitions to bear some initial good spiritual fruits if the apparition at least partially conveys some of Christ's truth. But a revelation that is either human or satanic in its origins cannot, for any sustained period, produce the kind of fruits that an authentic revelation does. The work of God and the work of man or Satan can never be comparable.

Degrees of Church Approval

After the Catholic Church has carefully reviewed the message, the surrounding phenomena, and the spiritual fruits of an alleged apparition, it will render judgment on the apparition. Historically, however, that judgment is not always a clear-cut decision. For example, regarding the reported Marian apparition at Knock, Ireland, in 1879, the Church gave for many years what, for lack of a better term, can be called "approval by omission." In other words, the Church never officially approved or disapproved of the apparition, but, first by not prohibiting the faithful from visiting the location of the apparition, then by the visits of Church officials (including John Paul II) to Knock, and then by acknowledging the Marian title of "Our Lady of Knock," it did eventually give its approval in an indirect way.

Other apparitions have received a higher type of approval, wherein the Church declares that there is nothing contrary to faith or morals in the revelation's message and that the faithful are free to believe in the truth of the apparition.

Still other apparitions have actually received a stronger level of approval, in which the local bishop issues a positive judgment about the apparition's authenticity. This happened with, among others, the Marian apparitions in 1932 and 1933 in Beauraing, Belgium; in 1987 in Betania, Venezuela; and in 2002 in Amsterdam, Holland.

Regardless of the level of approval an apparition receives from the Church, the faithful are never *obliged* to accept a Marian private revelation; only the public revelation contained in the deposit of faith is so binding on believers. Nevertheless, the fact that the Church grants some degree of approval to certain reported apparitions is a very good reason to accept their messages. This holds true even for non-Catholics, who are just as much the intended audience of their spiritual mother's words as Catholics.

And that brings us to our next question: what exactly are those words?

Mary's Message to the Modern World

As I mentioned earlier, over the past 200 years, the Catholic Church has approved more Marian apparitions than at any other point in its history. All of these approved apparitions, at their heart, have the same message: a call to penance and the conversion of hearts. The urgency and strength of that message, however, has grown ever greater as the decades have passed. A survey of some of the most important and universally recognized Marian apparitions should help make both the message and its urgency a little clearer.

The year 1830 is the beginning of what many Catholic scholars refer to as "the Marian Era" or the "Age of Mary." On November 27 of that year, Jesus' mother appeared to Catherine Labouré, a religious sister of the Daughters of Charity, at the order's motherhouse in Paris. There, Catherine saw Mary before her, standing on a globe and crushing a serpent beneath her feet. Rays of light, symbolizing the graces that come to us from Christ through Mary, streamed from her outstretched hands. Around the image of Mary, Catherine saw the following prayer written: "O Mary, conceived without sin, pray for us who have recourse to thee."

The vision was then turned around, revealing a cross linked to an M by a horizontal bar through the top of the M. Beneath the letter M were the hearts of Jesus and Mary, the former crowned with thorns and the latter pierced with a sword.[108] The entire image was also encircled with twelve stars.[109]

During the vision, Mary told the young nun, "Have a medal struck after this model. All who wear it will receive great graces. They should wear it around the neck."

Less than two years later, the Archbishop of Paris granted permission for the first medals to be struck. Those who wore the medals experienced so many spiritual and physical benefits that they began calling the medal "miraculous." A Church investigation in 1836 approved the apparition's authenticity and, in 1842, granted its approval to the wearing of the "miraculous medal."[110]

It's important to note that those who wear the medal around their neck, like those who wear the Brown Scapular, are not invoking any magical charm. The grace of Christ, not some sort of amulet, is responsible for any spiritual or physical benefits that come to the wearer. But, in wearing the medal, they are signifying their openness to receiving those graces, and by the grace of Christ, that medal becomes a material channel through which they can receive it.

LOURDES

When Mary appeared to Catherine Labouré, the call to repentance and conversion was a gentle one, implicitly contained in the words "pray for us who have recourse to thee." In the Marian apparition at Lourdes, France, twenty-eight years later, the call became much more forceful.

Between February 11 and July 16, 1858, Mary appeared eighteen times to fourteen-year-old Bernadette Soubirous in the small mountain town of Lourdes. Mary more than once commanded Bernadette to pray for sinners, prompting the girl to repeat aloud, "Penitence, penitence, penitence." Throughout all of the apparitions, Mary also called upon Christians to pray the Rosary. Most of the time, that call came by means of her actions, not her words: whenever she appeared to Bernadette, Mary herself was always holding a Rosary and fingering the beads. Bernadette herself felt a strong call to pray the Rosary and, at the beginning and end of each apparition, would pray it, along with the people who came to observe what was happening.

In the ninth apparition, one of those miraculous concurring phenomena that we mentioned earlier took place: the revelation of a miraculous spring. The following is Bernadette's account of the event:

> While I was in prayer, the Lady said to me in a friendly but serious voice, "Go, drink, and wash in the spring." As I did

not know where this spring was, and as I did not think the matter important, I went toward the river. The Lady called me back and signed to me with her finger to go under the grotto to the left; I obeyed, but I did not see any water. Not knowing where to get it from, I scratched the earth and the water came. I let it get a little clear of the mud, then I drank and washed.[111]

That very spring still flows today, and thousands of those who have washed in its waters have received miraculous cures for physical and spiritual ailments. Some of those physical cures are documented miracles that defy any scientific or medical explanation. Like the miracles Jesus worked during his earthly life, the healings that have taken place through this spring are not ends in themselves, but signs intended to encourage the faithful to accept and live the Gospel message. They are the most visible fruits among hundreds of thousands of invisible spiritual fruits that followed in the wake of the Marian apparitions at Lourdes over the course of the past 150 years.

Before we move on, there is one more message communicated by Mary to the young Bernadette that has a great deal of significance. During the sixteenth apparition, Bernadette felt an interior impulse to ask the Lady what her name was. She put the question to her three times before receiving a response. This is how she describes Mary's answer:

At the third request, her face became very serious, and she seemed to bow down in an attitude of humility. Then she joined her hands and raised them to her breast . . . She looked up to heaven . . . then slowly opening her hands and leaning forward toward me, she said in a voice vibrating with emotion: "I am the Immaculate Conception."

Those words not only confirmed the dogma of the Immaculate Conception, which had been defined four years earlier, but they constituted a personal revelation from Mary herself: a revelation of her own self-understanding that she is in some true sense immaculate by her very nature as God's supreme creation.

FATIMA

In 1917, Mary once more appeared to call for repentance and conversion. This time, however, her instructions were more specific still.

The apparitions at Fatima, Portugal, began in 1916, with a series of angelic visitations to three children: Lucia, age ten; Jacinta, age seven; and Francisco, age eight. Then, on May 13, 1917, Mary appeared to the same three children. She returned for the next six months on the thirteenth day of each month, except for in August, when she appeared on the nineteenth. The most informative of all the apparitions took place on July 13. This apparition included a vision of hell, a call for the daily praying of the Rosary for peace in the world, for making daily sacrifices for the conversion of souls, for the offering of Holy Communion in reparation for sins on five consecutive first Saturdays of the month, and for devotion to Mary's Immaculate Heart. Mary also warned the children of troubles to come if people did not respond to her instructions. These troubles included persecutions of the Church, world war, and the rise of Russian Communism throughout the world.

She went on, however, to offer words of hope to the children. She told them that through the consecration of Russia to her Immaculate Heart and through the acts of reparation, there would be peace.

On October 13, Mary appeared one last time to all three children, this time in the company of her husband, St. Joseph, and the child Jesus. After the family had blessed the children and after Mary had issued one final warning, saying, "Do not offend the Lord our God anymore because he is already so offended," a visible miraculous phenomenon occurred. Witnessed and confirmed by 70,000 onlookers, the sun appeared to dance in the sky, giving off various colors, and then approached the earth with great intensity, only to return later to its position in the sky.

Mary appeared one more time to Lucia alone in 1925, after Lucia had entered a convent in Spain. There, on December 10, she asked Lucia to make known to the world a devotion of reparation to her Immaculate Heart. This is the account from Lucia's diary:

> [T]he most holy virgin appeared to her, and by her side, elevated by a luminous cloud, was a child. The most holy virgin rested her hand on her shoulder, and as she did so, she showed her a heart encircled by thorns, which she was holding in her hand. At the same time the Child said:
>
> "Have compassion on the heart of your most holy mother, covered with thorns, with which ungrateful men pierce it at every moment, and there is no one to make an act of reparation to remove them."

Mary then went on to explain the First Five Saturdays Devotion, which consists of confessing one's sins, receiving Communion, praying five decades of the Rosary with the intention of making reparation to Mary's Immaculate Heart (which refers to prayer and sacrifices made in atonement for offenses and indifferences shown by others toward Mary's motherly love for all humanity), and "keeping [Mary] company for fifteen minutes, while meditating on the fifteen mysteries of the Rosary," with the intention of making reparation for the sins of the world on the first Saturday of five consecutive months. Mary promised to assist at death with the graces necessary for salvation those who would make the first Saturday devotion.[112]

Obviously, this is a fully Catholic devotion. But all Christians (and non-Christians too) can accept this invitation to pray the Rosary for world peace, and to patiently offer daily trials and sacrifices to atone for the pains experienced by a mother's heart. All of these acts are a way of imitating St. Paul's reflections on the role of suffering in the Mystical Body of Christ in Colossians 1:24.

CONTEMPORARY REPORTED MARIAN APPARITIONS

Since Fatima, an unprecedented number of Marian apparitions have taken place around the globe. Some have been approved by the Church; others remain under investigation. But, from the Marian apparitions in Cuapa, Nicaragua; Akita, Japan; Kibeho, Africa; Hrushiv, Ukraine; and many other places, the message of repentance and conversion has not changed.

In the small Bosnian town of Medjugorje, the message of repentance and conversion has taken on its clearest and most penetrating form to date.[113] Although still under Church investigation, the reported apparitions in Medjugorje have received strong unofficial approval from a number of Catholic bishops, priests, theologians, scientists, and lay faithful who have investigated the events there in light of authentic Church criteria. More than thirty million pilgrims have visited Medjugorje in the past quarter century. The present Church status regarding Medjugorje is that it is neither approved nor condemned, but Catholics are free to visit, pray, and discern.[114]

The apparitions themselves reportedly began on June 24, 1981, when Mary first appeared to six Croatian youths. At the time of the writing of this book, the apparitions are reportedly still occurring. The basic message of Medjugorje can be summed up in themes of faith, prayer, fasting, conversion, and peace.

According to the visionaries, Mary has also asked that faithful Christians pray more often and more devotedly. She often expresses this by calling for "prayer of the heart." In addition to calling Catholics to daily Mass and other types of eucharistic devotion, she has asked for the daily praying a decade of the Rosary , the frequent reading of the Bible, and a personal consecration of all peoples to Jesus' Sacred Heart and her Immaculate Heart. Several of the monthly messages (given on the twenty-fifth of each month) have simply been, "Pray, pray, pray." Since 1984, the messages have asked for stricter fasting on Wednesdays and Fridays, calling Christians back to the typical fasting practice of the early Church.[115]

Mary's greatest desire is always to see her children grow closer to Jesus. Accordingly, one of her most frequent admonitions in Medjugorje has been for Christians to repent of their sins and be reconciled to God and with one another. She has specifically asked for receiving the sacrament of Confession at least once a month.

Coupled with a request for penitence has been a call for peace — not primarily for peace from armed conflict, but for the spiritual peace of Christ in the heart of each believer. That kind of peace is the fruit of greater faith, greater prayer, greater fasting, and greater conversion. Only when that kind of interior peace reigns in the heart of men, is peace between families, neighbors, and countries a possibility, which is why the call for spiritual peace remains primary in the Medjugorje messages.

One final element of the apparitions in Medjugorje, like those in Fatima, is the warning of a world chastisement if men fail to heed Mary's warnings and turn away from sin. Despite that warning, however, the overall message of these apparitions is one of hope and peace.

Meet Mary

The most recently approved Church apparitions by the local bishop are the apparitions of the "Lady of All Nations," in Amsterdam, Holland. The seer, Ida Peerdeman, received a message from Mary calling us to pray a prayer so that the Holy Spirit would descend into the hearts of all nations, preserving them from "degeneration, disaster, and war." The message also conveys a heavenly call for the proclamation of the dogma of Mary Coredemptrix, Mediatrix, and Advocate, saying that through the proclamation of this truth about Mary and her three motherly roles, the "Triumph of the Immaculate Heart" prophesied at the Marian apparitions of Fatima would reach its full completion.[116]

∞

As I wrote at the beginning of this chapter, a healthy degree of skepticism is understandable, even desirable, when people claim to have received some form of private revelation from heaven. Remember, though, that the key words there are "healthy degree." For when faced with a legitimate supernatural revelation that proves consistent with Christian teaching and produces lasting spiritual fruits, the most healthful thing a believer can do is to listen to the message of the revelation and strive to live it out in his own life. After all, choosing to pray and do a little penance never hurt anyone. The same cannot be said for making the opposite choice.

Conclusion

A Faithful Mother

If you happen to be married, you know that spouses are package deals. In other words, on your wedding day, you get more than just the woman or man of your dreams; you also get a new family — including a mother-in-law.

Now, some people choose to love their mother-in-law, and some choose to hate her; some choose to listen to her, and some choose not to listen to her; some choose to spend time with her, and some choose to avoid her at all costs. Some choices are wise and good. Others are neither wise nor good. But, regardless of what is chosen, a choice must be made.

The same is true with our response to Mary, the mother of Jesus. Some men have chosen to love her, others to hate her; some to listen to her, others to ignore her; some to spend time with her, others to avoid her. But everyone, at one point or another, must make a choice about how to respond to her. It's impossible not to. After all, she is the woman who gave birth to the man whose life is the mark by which we measure time. She is the woman who has inspired more architecture, more art, and more poetry than any other woman to walk this earth. And she is the woman whom the great (and not Catholic) historian Kenneth Clark described as the "protectress of civilization, [who] taught a race of tough and ruthless barbarians the virtues of tenderness and compassion."[117] You

Meet Mary

can no more live in this world of ours and ignore Mary than you can choose to ignore the mother of the person you marry.

This book, from start to finish, has been about the way one group of Mary's children has chosen to respond to her and, in that response, how they have come to understand her. Other books could be written by Muslims, who revere her as a godly woman and a model of virtue, or by radical feminists, who revile her as a symbol of feminine passivity and submissiveness. Still more books could have been written by New Age gurus who see Mary as an icon of the sacred feminine or as an incarnation of the primordial earth goddess. But, as with the choices we make with our earthly mothers and mothers-in-law, all responses to Mary are not created equal.

That's because Mary is a person, not an idea. She's a real woman, not a myth or a symbol. And for two millennia, Christians have been saying who this real woman is: the mother of our Lord and the mother of all men. From the opening pages of Genesis, where the Lord promised Adam and Eve that one day a woman would be born who would stand in total enmity to Satan, to the closing pages of Revelation, where St. John saw a woman, clothed with the sun, doing battle with Satan for the souls of her spiritual children, the Bible attests to the importance of Mary in salvation history. The prayers and the teachings of the early Church echo the Bible, and in the four defined Marian dogmas of the Catholic Church, those teachings have their full flowering. Mary is the Mother of God, the Perpetual Virgin, the Immaculate Conception, and the Assumed Queen of Heaven.

Her spiritual motherhood to us, often expressed in the Catholic Church under the titles Co-redemptrix, Mediatrix, and Advocate, is a real motherhood. It helps give new life to our souls, helps sustain that life through prayer, and nourishes us with the graces that come through her hands from Christ, her son. As a uniquely holy mother, she also models for us what it means to live the life of grace in all its fullness. She shows us, through her total obedience to the Father's will, her total receptivity to the Holy Spirit, and her total devotion to her Son, what it means to be a true disciple.

The truth of who Mary is and what she does is not dependent on our recognition of that truth or our response to her. But, when we respond to her rightly, when we give her the love, honor, and devotion she deserves, we permit her to mother us with the full power of her motherly heart. Through seeking her prayers and her counsel, as well as through meditating with her on the mysteries of her son's life, we allow her to draw us ever closer to her Son, the source of all the grace she has been blessed with and with which she in turn blesses us.

And that, as I've already said so many times in this book, is what devotion to Mary is all about. We love her as our mother and let her love us as a mother, so that through that mutual exchange of love, we might be drawn ever more deeply into the love of Christ. Everything Mary does, everything she is, is ordered to her son, to bringing souls to him. She could never be satisfied with love from her children that ended in love for only her. Rather, she seeks a love that goes beyond her, to the one who created her. And she will settle for nothing less.

I don't expect all of the readers of this book to agree with or like everything the Catholic Church teaches about Mary. At least not right away. But, again, I didn't write this book to argue for those teachings, but to attest to them. I wrote it to give you a picture of a woman whom millions of men and women through the centuries have loved more dearly than their own mothers. What you choose to do with this picture is up to you. But do not look away as soon as you put this book down. Continue to gaze upon her face. Look in her eyes. Ask her what she can tell you about suffering, compassion, grace, obedience, and love. And most important, ask her what she can tell you about her son, Jesus. She will answer. She is, after all and above all, a faithful mother to him and to us.

Appendix

The Rosary
and Other Marian Prayers

Following are the basic components of the Rosary, including its structure and order, and the prayers and Mysteries of the Rosary, accompanied by a brief Scripture verse pertaining to the respective Gospel mystery.

The Structure of the Rosary

The Rosary is a form of vocal and mental prayer on the mysteries of our Redemption, divided into twenty decades. The recitation of each decade is accompanied by meditation on one of the twenty events or "mysteries."

The Sign of the Cross and the Apostles' Creed
Our Father
Three Hail Marys
Glory Be; announce first Mystery.
Our Father
Ten Hail Marys; meditate on the mystery announced.
Glory Be and optional "Fatima Prayer."

Announce the next Mystery and repeat an Our Father, ten Hail Marys, a Glory Be and an optional Fatima Prayer.

Hail, Holy Queen and Rosary Prayer; end with the Sign of the Cross.

The Twenty Mysteries of the Rosary

JOYFUL MYSTERIES

(prayed on Mondays and Saturdays)

1. *The Annunciation:* "Hail, full of grace, the Lord is with you."[118]

2. *The Visitation:* "When Elizabeth heard the greeting of Mary, the babe leaped in her womb; and Elizabeth was filled with the Holy Spirit."[119]

3. *The Birth of Jesus:* "And she gave birth to her first-born son and wrapped Him in swaddling clothes."[120]

4. *The Presentation:* ". . . According to the law of Moses, they brought [Jesus] up to Jerusalem to present him to the Lord."[121]

5. *The Finding of the Child Jesus in the Temple:* "After three days, they found him in the Temple, sitting among the teachers."[122]

LUMINOUS MYSTERIES

(prayed on Thursdays)

6. *The Baptism of the Lord:* "This is my beloved Son, with whom I am well pleased."[123]

7. *The Wedding at Cana:* "His mother said to the servants, 'Do whatever he tells you.' "[124]

8. *The Proclamation of the Kingdom of God:* "The kingdom of God is at hand; repent, and believe in the gospel."[125]

9. *The Transfiguration:* "As he was praying, the appearance of his countenance was altered, and his raiment became dazzling white. And behold, two men talked with him, Moses and Elijah, who appeared in glory and spoke of his departure, which he was to accomplish at Jerusalem."[126]

10. *The Institution of the Eucharist:* "And he took bread, and when he had given thanks, he broke it and gave it to them, saying, 'This is my body which is given for you. Do this in remembrance of me.' "[127]

SORROWFUL MYSTERIES
(prayed on Tuesdays and Fridays)

11. *The Agony in the Garden:* "Jesus went with them to a place called Gethsemane . . . He began to be sorrowful and troubled."[128]

12. *The Scourging at the Pillar:* "Then Pilate took Jesus and scourged him."[129]

13. *The Crowning with Thorns:* "And plaiting a crown of thorns, they put it upon his head, and put a reed into his right hand."[130]

14. *Jesus Carries the Cross:* ". . . And he went out, bearing his own cross, to the place called the place of a skull."[131]

15. *The Crucifixion:* "And when they came to the place which is called The Skull, there they crucified him."[132]

GLORIOUS MYSTERIES
(prayed on Sundays and Wednesdays)

16. *The Resurrection:* "He is not here, but has risen. See the place where they laid him."[133]

17. *The Ascension:* "The Lord Jesus . . . was taken up into heaven, and sat down at the right hand of God."[134]

18. *The Descent of the Holy Spirit:* "And suddenly a sound came from Heaven . . . And there appeared to them tongues as of fire . . . And they were all filled with the Holy Spirit."[135]

19. *The Assumption of Mary, Body and Soul, into Heaven:* "Hear, O daughter, and consider, and incline your ear . . . the king will desire your beauty . . . The princess is decked in her chamber with gold-woven robes; in many-colored robes she is led to the king."[136]

20. *The Coronation of Mary, Queen of Heaven and Earth:* "And a great portent appeared in heaven, a woman clothed with the sun, with the moon under her feet, and on her head a crown of twelve stars."[137]

How to Pray the Rosary

The Rosary begins by holding the Cross and making the Sign of the Cross as we pray:

THE SIGN OF THE CROSS
In the name of the Father, and of the Son, and of the Holy Spirit. Amen.

The Rosary and Other Marian Prayers

While still holding the Cross, we profess our beliefs as we pray:

THE APOSTLES' CREED
I believe in God, the Father Almighty,
Creator of Heaven and earth;
and in Jesus Christ, His only Son, our Lord;
Who was conceived by the Holy Spirit, born of the Virgin Mary,
Suffered under Pontius Pilate, was crucified, died, and was buried.
He descended into Hell; the third day He rose again from the dead;
He ascended into Heaven, sits at the right hand
of God, the Father Almighty;
from thence He shall come to judge the living and the dead.
I believe in the Holy Spirit, the holy Catholic Church,
the Communion of Saints, the forgiveness of sins,
the resurrection of the body, and life everlasting. Amen.

On the first bead we pray the Our Father. This is traditionally offered for the intention of the Holy Father, the Pope:

OUR FATHER
Our Father, who art in Heaven,
hallowed be Thy name;
Thy kingdom come;
Thy will be done on earth, as it is in Heaven.
Give us this day our daily bread;
and forgive us our trespasses,
as we forgive those who trespass against us;
and lead us not into temptation,
but deliver us from evil. Amen.

Three Hail Marys are then prayed for the virtues of faith, hope, and charity:

Meet Mary

HAIL MARY

Hail, Mary, full of grace; the Lord is with thee;
blessed art thou among women,
and blessed is the fruit of thy womb, Jesus.
Holy Mary, Mother of God, pray for us sinners,
now and at the hour of our death. Amen.

We then pray the Glory Be (no bead):

GLORY BE

Glory be to the Father, and to the Son, and to the Holy Spirit.
As it was in the beginning, is now,
and ever shall be, world without end. Amen.

On the fifth bead, we announce the First Mystery and, while meditating on the mystery, say one Our Father and ten Hail Marys (one on each of the next ten beads) and a Glory Be (no bead). Then, as requested by Our Lady of the Rosary at Fatima, we pray:

FATIMA PRAYER

O my Jesus, forgive us our sins,
save us from the fires of Hell.
Lead all souls to Heaven, especially those
who are most in need of thy mercy.

On the next bead, announce the Second Mystery, and repeat this sequence for each mystery.

At the end of the five decades, the Hail, Holy Queen is prayed:

HAIL, HOLY QUEEN

Hail! Holy Queen, Mother of Mercy,
our life, our sweetness, and our hope.

To thee do we cry, poor banished children of Eve;
to thee do we send up our sighs,
mourning and weeping in this valley of tears.
Turn, then, most gracious advocate,
thine eyes of mercy toward us; and after this our exile,
show unto us the blessed fruit of thy womb, Jesus.
O clement, O loving, O sweet Virgin Mary.
V. *Pray for us, O holy Mother of God.*
R. *That we may be made worthy of the promises of Christ.*

OPTIONAL CLOSING PRAYER
FROM THE ROMAN MISSAL
O God, whose only-begotten Son, by His life, death,
and Resurrection, has purchased for us the reward of eternal life;
grant, we beseech you, that, while meditating on these
Mysteries of the most holy Rosary of the Blessed Virgin Mary,
we may imitate what they contain and obtain what they promise.
Through the same Christ our Lord. Amen.

End with the Sign of the Cross.

Other Marian Prayers

ANGELUS
V. *The angel of the Lord declared unto Mary.*
R. *And she conceived by the Holy Spirit.*

Hail Mary . . .

V. *Behold the handmaid of the Lord.*
R. *Be it done unto me according to your word.*

Hail Mary . . .

V. *And the Word was made flesh.*
R. *And dwelt among us.*

Hail Mary . . .

Let us pray: Pour forth we beseech thee, O Lord, your grace
into our hearts, that we to whom the Incarnation of Christ, your son,
was made known by the message of an angel, may, by his
Passion and Cross, be brought to the glory of his Resurrection,
through the same Christ Our Lord. Amen.

MEMORARE
Remember, O most gracious Virgin Mary,
that never was it known that anyone who fled to your protection
implored your help, or sought your intercession was left unaided.
Inspired with this confidence, I fly to you, O virgin of virgins,
my mother; to you do I come, before you I stand, sinful and sorrowful.

O mother of the Word Incarnate, despise not my petitions,
but, in your mercy, hear and answer me.

REGINA CAELI
(replaces the *Angelus* during the Easter Season)
Queen of Heaven, rejoice, alleluia:
For He whom you merited to bear, alleluia,
Has risen, as He said, alleluia.
Pray for us to God, alleluia.
V. Rejoice and be glad, O Virgin Mary, alleluia.
R. Because the Lord is truly risen, alleluia.

Let us pray. O God, who, by the Resurrection of your son,
our Lord Jesus Christ, granted joy to the whole world:
grant, we beg you, that through the intercession of the

The Rosary and Other Marian Prayers

Virgin Mary, His mother, we may lay hold of the joys of eternal life. Through the same Christ our Lord. Amen.

AVE MARIS STELLA
Hail, O Star of the ocean,
God's own Mother blest,
ever sinless Virgin,
gate of heav'nly rest.

Taking that sweet Ave,
which from Gabriel came,
peace confirm within us,
changing Eve's name.

Break the sinners' fetters,
make our blindness day,
Chase all evils from us,
for all blessings pray.

Show thyself a Mother,
may the Word divine
born for us thine Infant
hear our prayers through thine.

Virgin all excelling,
mildest of the mild,
free from guilt preserve us
meek and undefiled.

Keep our life all spotless,
make our way secure
till we find in Jesus,
joy for evermore.

Praise to God the Father,
honor to the Son,
in the Holy Spirit,
be the glory one. Amen.

FATIMA PRAYERS

My God, I believe, I adore, I hope, and I love you!
I beg pardon of you for those who do not believe,
do not adore, do not hope, and do not love you.

Most Holy Trinity, Father, Son, and Holy Spirit,
I adore you profoundly and offer you the most precious
Body, Blood, Soul, and Divinity of Jesus Christ,
present in all the tabernacles of the world, in reparation
for the outrages, sacrileges and indifferences
by which he is offended. And through the infinite merits of his most
Sacred Heart and the Immaculate Heart of Mary,
I beg of you the conversion of poor sinners.

THE LITANY OF THE BLESSED VIRGIN MARY

Lord, have mercy.
Christ, have mercy.
Lord, have mercy.
Christ, hear us.
Christ, graciously hear us.

God, the Father of Heaven,
have mercy on us.
God the Son, Redeemer of the world,
have mercy on us.
God the Holy Spirit, have mercy on us.
Holy Trinity, one God, have mercy on us.

The Rosary and Other Marian Prayers

Holy Mary, *pray for us.*
Mother of Christ, *pray for us.*
Mother of the Church, *pray for us.*
Mother of divine grace, *pray for us.*
Mother most pure, *pray for us.*
Mother most chaste, *pray for us.*
Mother inviolate, *pray for us.*
Mother undefiled, *pray for us.*
Mother most amiable, *pray for us.*
Mother most admirable, *pray for us.*
Mother of good counsel, *pray for us.*
Mother of our creator, *pray for us.*
Mother of our savior, *pray for us.*
Virgin most prudent, *pray for us.*
Virgin most venerable, *pray for us.*
Virgin most renowned, *pray for us.*
Virgin most powerful, *pray for us.*
Virgin most merciful, *pray for us.*
Virgin most faithful, *pray for us.*
Mirror of justice, *pray for us.*
Seat of wisdom, *pray for us.*
Cause of our joy, *pray for us.*
Spiritual vessel, *pray for us.*
Vessel of honor, *pray for us.*
Singular vessel of devotion, *pray for us.*
Mystical rose, *pray for us.*
Tower of David, *pray for us.*
Tower of ivory, *pray for us.*
House of gold, *pray for us.*
Ark of the covenant, *pray for us.*
Gate of Heaven, *pray for us.*

Morning star, pray for us.
Health of the sick, pray for us.
Refuge of sinners, pray for us.
Comforter of the afflicted, pray for us.
Help of Christians, pray for us.
Queen of angels, pray for us.
Queen of patriarchs, pray for us.
Queen of prophets, pray for us.
Queen of apostles, pray for us.
Queen of martyrs, pray for us.
Queen of confessors, pray for us.
Queen of virgins, pray for us.
Queen of all saints, pray for us.
Queen conceived without Original Sin, pray for us.
Queen assumed into heaven, pray for us.
Queen of the most holy Rosary, pray for us.
Queen of the family, pray for us.
Queen of peace, pray for us.

Lamb of God,
You take away the sins of the world;
spare us, O Lord.
Lamb of God,
You take away the sins of the world;
graciously hear us, O Lord.
Lamb of God,
You take away the sins of the world;
have mercy on us.

V. *Pray for us, O Holy Mother of God.*
R. *That we may be made worthy*
of the promises of Christ.

Let us pray. Grant, we beg you, O Lord God,
that we your servants may enjoy lasting health of mind and body,
and by the glorious intercession of the Blessed Mary, ever virgin,
be delivered from present sorrow and enter into
the joy of eternal happiness.
Through Christ our Lord. Amen.

TOTAL CONSECRATION PRAYER
TO JESUS THROUGH MARY
by St. Louis de Montfort

O Eternal and Incarnate Wisdom! O sweetest and most adorable Jesus! True God and true man, only son of the eternal Father, and of Mary, always virgin! I adore you profoundly in the bosom and splendors of your Father during eternity; and I adore you also in the virginal bosom of Mary, your most worthy Mother, in the time of your Incarnation.

I give you thanks that you have annihilated yourself, taking the form of a slave in order to rescue me from the cruel slavery of the Devil. I praise and glorify you because you have been pleased to submit yourself to Mary, your holy Mother, in all things, in order to make me your faithful slave through her. But, alas! Ungrateful and faithless as I have been, I have not kept the promises which I made so solemnly to you in my Baptism; I have not fulfilled my obligations; I do not deserve to be called your child, nor yet your slave; and as there is nothing in me which does not merit your anger and your repulse, I dare not come by myself before your most holy and august Majesty. It is on this account that I have recourse to the intercession of your most holy Mother, whom you have given me for a Mediatrix with you. It is through her that I hope to obtain from you contrition, the pardon of my sins, and the acquisition and preservation of wisdom.

Meet Mary

Hail, then, O Immaculate Mary, living tabernacle of the Divinity, where the Eternal Wisdom willed to be hidden and to be adored by angels and by men! Hail, O Queen of heaven and earth, to whose empire everything is subject which is under God. Hail, O sure refuge of sinners, whose mercy fails no one. Hear the desires which I have of the Divine Wisdom; and for that end, receive the vows and offerings which in my lowliness I present to you.

I, (Name), a faithless sinner, renew and ratify today in your hands the vows of my Baptism; I renounce forever Satan, his pomps and works; and I give myself entirely to Jesus Christ, the Incarnate Wisdom, to carry my cross after him all the days of my life, and to be more faithful to him than I have ever been before.

In the presence of all the heavenly court, I choose you this day for my Mother and Queen. I deliver and consecrate to you, as your slave, my body and soul, my goods, both interior and exterior, and even the value of all my good actions, past, present and future; leaving to you the entire and full right of disposing of me, and all that belongs to me, without exception, according to your good pleasure, for the greater glory of God, in time and in eternity. Receive, O gracious Virgin, this little offering of my slavery, in honor of, and in union with, that subjection which the Eternal Wisdom deigned to have to your maternity, in homage to the power which both of you have over this poor sinner, and in thanksgiving for the privileges with which the Holy Trinity has favored you. I declare that I wish henceforth, as your true slave, to seek your honor and to obey you in all things.

O admirable Mother, present me to your dear son as his eternal slave, so that as he has redeemed me by you, by you he may receive me! O Mother of mercy, grant me the grace to obtain the true wisdom of God; and for that end, receive me among those whom you love and teach, whom you lead, nourish and protect as your children and your slaves.

O faithful Virgin, make me in all things so perfect a disciple, imitator and slave of the Incarnate Wisdom, Jesus Christ, your son, that I may attain, by your intercession and by your example, to the fullness of his age on earth and of his glory in heaven. Amen.

Endnotes

1   These models are taken from *Ineffabilis Deus*, Pius IX, 1854.

2   Luke 1:26-38.

3   Luke 1:39-56.

4   Luke 2:7.

5   Matt. 1:18.

6   Matt. 2:1-13.

7   Matt. 2:13-18.

8   Matt. 2:19-23.

9   John 2:1-11.

10 John 19:25-27.

11 Acts 1:13-2:4.

12 Gal. 4:4.

13 Rev. 12:1.

14 Rev. 12:5.

15 Rev. 12:17.

[16] Gen. 3:15. Although some translations have the pronoun *she* for the one crushing the serpent's head, the original Hebrew somewhat favors the masculine *he*. But in either case, the victory over Satan is ultimately that of Jesus Christ with Mary's instrumental participation as the "New Eve."

For a defense of the *she* pronoun from historical and medieval commentaries, particularly Cornelius à Lapide, cf. Br. Thomas Sennott, M.I.C.M., "Mary Co-redemptrix," *Mary at the Foot of the Cross II: Acts of the International Symposium on Marian Coredemption* (Academy of the Immaculate, 2002), 49-63. The author offers the following initial explanation in support of *ipsa* and quotes Cornelius à Lapide in support:

In Hebrew *hu* is "he," and *he* "she" . . . There is no "it" in Hebrew, both *hu* and *he* can be translated "it" depending on the context.

In Greek "he" is *autos*, "she" *aute*, and "it" *auto*.

In Latin "he" is *ipse*, "she" *ipsa*, and "it" *ipsum* . . .

Cornelius à Lapide, in his great *Commentaria in Scripturam Sacram*, says that the underlying mystery is even reflected in the Hebrew grammar. "Also *hu* is often used instead of *he* especially when there is some emphasis on action and something manly is predicated of the woman, as is the case here with the crushing of the serpent's head . . . It makes no difference that the verb is masculine *yasuph*, that is, "[he] shall crush," for it often happens in Hebrew that the masculine is used instead of the feminine and vice versa, especially when there is an underlying reason or mystery, as I have just said" (C. à Lapide, *Commentaria in Scripturam Sacram* [Larousse, Paris, 1848], 105). The "underlying mystery" is, of course, that our Lady crushes the head of the serpent by the power of our Lord.

[17] Gen. 28:12.

[18] Exod. 3:1.

[19] 1 Kings 8.

[20] Gen. 6:14; Exod. 37:1.

[21] Cf. John 1:14.

[22] Cf. John 6:35.

[23] Cf. Heb. 4:14.

[24] For more information on Mary in the early Church, see J. Murphy, "Origin and Nature of Marian Cult" in J. B. Carol, O.F.M., ed., *Mariology*, Vol. III (Milwaukee: Bruce, 1961).

[25] St. Justin Martyr, *Dialogue with Trypho*, ch. 100, *Patrologia Graeca (PG)*, Migne, 6, 709-712.

[26] St. Irenaeus, *Adversus haereses*, Bk. 3, 1; PG 7, 958-959.

[27] St. Ambrose, *Epist.* 63, n. 33, *Patrologia Latina (PL)*, Migne, 16, 1249-1250; Sermon 45, n. 4; *PL* 17, 716.

[28] St. Jerome, *Epist.* 22, n. 21, *PL* 22, 408.

[29] Cf. W. Burghart, S.J., "Mary in Western Patristic Thought," *Mariology*, Vol. I, 1955; Murphy, *Mariology*, Vol. III.

[30] For a more detailed study of Mary's Divine Motherhood, see G. van Ackeren, S.J., "Mary's Divine Motherhood" in *Mariology*, Vol. II, 1957 and J. B. Carol, O.F.M., *Fundamentals of Mariology* (New York: Benzinger Bros., 1957), 35-40.

[31] Cf. St. Ignatius of Antioch, *Ad Eph.* 19, 1: AF 11/2 76-80.

[32] Denzinger's *Enchiridion Symbolorum (DS)*, 256.

[33] Luke 1:27.

[34] Luke 1:34.

[35] Luke 1:35.

[36] St. Augustine, *Serm.* 189, n. 2; *PL* 38, 1005.

[37] Pope St. Leo, *Enchiridion Patristicum (EP)* 2182.

[38] St. Thomas Aquinas, *Summa Theologica*, III, Q. 28, art. 2. It follows that Mary's giving birth to Jesus would be a painless experience, since pain in childbirth is a punitive effect of Original Sin (cf. Gen 3:15). Mary, being free from the penalty of Original Sin due to her Immaculate Conception, would likewise be free from the penalty of a painful process of childbirth. For a more detailed study, see Carol, *Fundamentals*, 147, and Carol, "Mary's Virginity in Partu," *Homiletic and Pastoral Review*, 54, 1954.

[39] Matt. 12:46, 13:55; Mark 3:31.

[40] Gen. 13:8.

[41] Gen. 29:15.

[42] Mark 6:3.

[43] *DS* 214; cf. Burghart, "Mary in Eastern Patristic Thought," *Mariology*, Vol. II. For a more detailed study of whether Mary took a vow of virginity, see Collins, S.J., "Our Lady's Vow of Virginity" in *Catholic Biblical Quarterly*, 5, 1943.

[44] St. Thomas Aquinas, *Summa Theologica*, III, Q. 28, art. 3.

[45] One of the principal objections to the Immaculate Conception in the scholastic age was based on the misunderstood notion of how Original Sin was transmitted. Since they erroneously held that Original Sin was transmitted from an infected body to the soul once the soul was created and infused, then Mary would have contracted Original Sin from the fallen nature of St. Anne, her mother. It was Blessed Duns Scotus who correctly clarified that Original Sin consisted rather in the absence of sanctifying grace in the soul at conception, a deprivation caused by the sin of Adam and Eve. Hence, Mary, by the merits of Jesus Christ, was granted that gift of sanctifying grace in her soul at conception.

[46] Again, although some translations have the pronoun *he* and some *she* for the one crushing the serpent's head, the victory over Satan is ultimately that of Jesus Christ with Mary's instrumental participation as the "New Eve."

[47] Luke 1:26-38.

[48] Cf. Pius IX, *Ineffabilis Deus*, 1854.

[49] St. Ephraem, *Sermones exegetici, opera omnia syriace et latine*, 2, Rome, 1740, 327.

[50] St. Ambrose, *Exposito in Psalm* 118, Sermon 22, n. 30, *PL* 15, 1599. St. Severus, *Hom., cathedralis*, 67, *Patrologia Orientalis (PO)* 8, 350. St. Sophronius, *Oral in Deiparae Annunt.*, 25, *PG* 87, 3246-3247. St. Andrew, *Hom. 1 in Nativ. Deiparae*, *PG* 97, 913-914.

[51] St. Gregory of Tours, *Libri miraculorum*, Bk. I, ch. 4; *PL* 71, 708. For additional information, see Carol, Fundamentals, 188.

[52] Cf. Pius XII, *Munificentissimus Deus*, 1950.

[53] John 19:26-27.

[54] Cf. St. Augustine, *De S. Virginitate* 6, 6. At least twenty-eight popes have also taught that Mary is our spiritual mother. For more information, see Carol, *Fundamentals*, 48.

[55] John 19:27. That John represents all humanity and especially all disciples, cf. John Paul II, *Redemptoris Mater*, 23, 45, and Leo XIII, *Adiutricem*.

[56] For a more detailed study of Mary's spiritual motherhood, see Mark Miravalle, *Mary: Coredemptrix, Mediatrix, Advocate* (Santa Barbara: Queenship, 1993), and Mark Miravalle, *"With Jesus": The Story of Mary, Coredemptrix* (Santa Barbara: Queenship, 2003).

[57] Cf. 1 Cor. 3:9.

[58] Luke 2:25.

[59] Rev. 12:5, 2.

[60] St. Irenaeus, *Adversus haereses*, Bk. 3, 32, 1; PG 7, 958-959. Epiphanius, *Haer.* 78, 18: PG 42, 728CD-729AB. St. Jerome, *Epist.* 22, n. 21, PL 22, 408. John Paul II, *Redemptoris Mater*, 23.

[61] Luke 2:19, 51.

[62] St. Cyril of Alexandria, *Hom. in Deiparam*, PG 65. St. Germain of Constantinople, *Hom. in Dorm.* II, PG 98, 321, 352-3. St. Peter Damien, *Serm.* 44, PL 144, 740. St. Ephraem, *Oratio* IV, *Ad Deiparam*.

[63] 1 Tim. 2:5.

[64] 1 Tim. 2:1-2.

65 St. Irenaeus, *Adversus haereses*, Bk. 5, 19, *PG* 1175-1176; St. Ephraem, *S. Ephraem Syri testim. de B.V.M. mediatione, Ephemerides Theologicae Lovanienses*, IV, fasc. 2, 1927.

66 John 2.

67 For further distinction of *latria, dulia,* and *hyperdulia,* see St. Thomas Aquinas, *Summa Theologica*, II-II, Q. 84, art. 1; Q. 304, art. 1-4.

68 Luke 2:52.

69 The Blessed Virgin Mary alone had an "intrinsic relationship with the Hypostatic Union": Suarez, S.J., *Disputationes*, 10.

70 Pope John Paul II, *Angelus* message, October 29, 1978.

71 Luke 2:19.

72 Luke 1:26.

73 Luke 1:39.

74 Luke 2:7, Matt. 1:25.

75 Luke 2:21.

76 Luke 2:42.

77 Matt. 3:13.

78 John 2:1.

79 Matt. 4:17.

80 Luke 9:28.

81 1 Cor. 11:23.

[82] Matt. 26:36.

[83] John 19:1.

[84] Matt. 27:29.

[85] John 19:17.

[86] Luke 23:33.

[87] Luke 24:6.

[88] Mark 16:19.

[89] Acts 2:2.

[90] Ps. 131:8; Gen. 3:15; Luke 1:28.

[91] Rev. 12:1.

[92] It was in the Apostolic Constitution *Consueverant Romani Pontifices* that Pope St. Pius V approved the basic form of the Rosary, and it was in the Apostolic Letter *Rosarium Virginis Mariae*, in 2002, that Pope John Paul II introduced the Luminous Mysteries to the Rosary.

[93] Pope Paul VI in his Apostolic Exhortation *Marialis Cultus* refers to the Rosary as "the compendium of the entire Gospel" and emphasizes its Christocentric nature (42, 46).

[94] Luke 11:2; Matt. 6:7.

[95] St. Louis Marie de Montfort strongly emphasized the value of physically fingering the beads while in spiritual conversation with God during Rosary prayer. Cf. *Secret of the Rosary*, ch. 1-3.

[96] P. M. Xiberta, O. Carm., *De Visione Sancti Simonis Stock* (Rome, 1950). Cf. Christian Ceroke, O. Carm., "The Scapular

Devotion," *Mariology*, Vol. III. Pope Pius XII spoke of the powerful spiritual effects of wearing the scapular in the following discourse: "How many souls, even in circumstances which, humanly speaking, were beyond hope, have owed their final conversion and their eternal salvation to the Scapular which they were wearing! How many more, thanks to it, have experienced the motherly protection of Mary in dangers of body and soul" (*Discourses and Radio Broadcasts*, Vol. 12, 1950-51.

[97] St. John Damascene (d. 749), referred to himself as a "slave of the Mother of God" and authored the following prayer form of Marian consecration in the eighth century: "O Lady, before you we take our stand. Lady, I call you Virgin Mother of God and to your hope, as to the sure and strongest anchor we bind ourselves; to you we consecrate our mind, our soul, our body, all that we are . . ." (*Hom. I in dorm.*, in *PG* 96, 720A). Even before St. Damascene, the phrase *servus Mariae* ("servant or slave of Mary") can be found in African sermons from the fifth and the sixth centuries. The Western saint Idlefonsus of Toledo (d. 669), also wrote of being "the servant of the handmaid of the Lord" (*De virginitate sanctae Mariae*, ed., V. G. Blance, Madrid, 1937). Cf. M. O'Carroll, C.S.Sp. "Consecration," *Theotokos: A Theological Encyclopedia of the Blessed Virgin Mary* (Michael Glazier, Inc., 1983), 109.

[98] De Montfort, *True Devotion*, no. 257.

[99] For a more in-depth study of private revelation, see Mark Miravalle, *Private Revelation: Discerning with the Church* (Santa Barbara: Queenship, 2007). The definitive study of private revelation and its concurring mystical phenomena is generally accepted to be the five-volume work in Latin by Pope Benedict XIV (written while he was Cardinal Prospero Lambertini),

De Servorum Dei Beatificatione et de Beatorum Canonizatione (1734-1738). Portions of this monumental work are available in English in a three-volume translation entitled *Heroic Virtue: A Portion of the Treatise of Benedict XIV on the Beatification and Canonization of the Servants of God.*

[100] An example of private revelation serving to call the Church to concentrate more on a specific Gospel truth is that of the private revelations of Divine Mercy to St. Faustina Kowalska in the 1930s, which led the Church to accentuate even more profoundly the scriptural and traditional teaching of God's infinite mercy for our present day.

[101] St. Thomas Aquinas, *Summa Theologica*, II-II, Q. 174, art. 6, ad. 3.

[102] For example, see 1 Cor. 12:10; Rom. 12:6; Eph. 4:11.

[103] Joel 2:28.

[104] Acts 21:9-10.

[105] For further study into the nature and various forms of visions and locutions, see St. John of the Cross, *The Ascent of Mount Camel*, Bk. II. For discussion of Church criteria for evaluating an alleged private revelation, see R. Laurentin, *The Role of Apparitions in the Life of the Church*, presentation at National Conference on Medjugorje (Notre Dame University, May 12, 1989).

[106] For information concerning the studies done on the visionaries of Medjugorje, see R. Laurentin and H. Joyeux, *Scientific and Medical Studies in the Apparitions at Medjugorje* (Lancaster, Pennsylvania: Veritas Press, 1987).

[107] Matt. 12:33.

[108] Cf. Luke 2:35.

[109] Cf. Rev. 12:1.

[110] For more information on the apparitions to St. Catherine Labouré, see the definitive English-language account of the apparitions and messages by J. Dirvin, C.M., *Saint Catherine Labouré of the Miraculous Medal* (TAN, 1984), ch. III, 36; see also R. Laurentin, *The Life of Catherine Labouré*, Collins Liturgical Publications, 1983. For the extensive French documentation of the messages and surrounding phenomena, see R. Laurentin, *Catherine Labouré et la Médaille Miraculeuse*, 2 vols. (Paris, 1976); R. Laurentin, *Vie Authentique de Ste. Catherine Labouré*, 2 vols. (Paris, 1980).

[111] This quotation and all other quotations of Bernadette Soubirous and accounts of Lourdes have been taken from J. B. Estrade, J. H. Girolestone, trans., *The Appearance of the Blessed Virgin Mary at the Grotto of Lourdes* (London: Art and Book Co., Ltd., 1912); see also Alan Heame, *The Happenings at Lourdes*, Catholic Book Club, 1968. For an exhaustive study and historical account of the apparitions at Lourdes, cf. R. Laurentin, *Lourdes. Histoire Authentique*, 6 vols., P. Lethielleux, Paris, 1961-1964 and R. Laurentin & Bernard Billet, O.S.B., *Lourdes: Documents Authentiques*, 7 vols. (P. Lethielleux, Paris, 1957-1966).

[112] For greater detail on the apparitions of Mary at Fatima, see M. Martins, S. J. & R. Fox, *Documents on Fatima and the Memoirs of Sister Lucia* (Fatima Family Apostolate, 2002).

[113] For a more complete introduction to the messages and apparitions of Medjugorje, see Mark Miravalle, *Introduction to Medjugorje* (Santa Barbara: Queenship, 2004).

114 For an excellent overview of the current Church status of the apparitions of Medjugorje, cf. Denis Nolan, *Medjugorje and the Church*, fourth edition (Santa Barbara: Queenship, 2007).

115 Didache 8:1.

116 For a complete collection of the messages given by the Lady of All Nations, see *The Messages of the Lady of All Nations* (The Lady of All Nations Foundation, 1999).

117 K. Clark, *Civilization*, as quoted in D. Lyons, *The Role of Mary Through the Centuries* (World Apostolate of Fatima).

118 Luke 1:28.

119 Luke 1:41.

120 Luke 2:7.

121 Luke 2:22.

122 Luke 2:46.

123 Matt. 3:17.

124 John 2:5.

125 Mark 1:15.

126 Luke 9:29-31.

127 Luke 22:19.

128 Matt. 26:36, 37.

129 John 19:1.

130 Matt. 27:29.

[131] John 19:17.

[132] Luke 23:33.

[133] Luke 24:5; Mark 16:6.

[134] Mark 16:19.

[135] Acts 2:2, 3, 4.

[136] Ps. 45:11, 12, 14.

[137] Rev. 12:1.

Mark Miravalle

Dr. Mark Miravalle, husband, permanent deacon, and father of eight, earned his Bachelor of Arts in Theology at the University of San Francisco. He is also a graduate of the St. Ignatius Institute Catholic Great Books Program, University of San Francisco, and has earned his Sacred Theological Doctorate at the Pontifical University of St. Thomas Aquinas in Rome.

Dr. Miravalle has been teaching at the Franciscan University of Steubenville since 1986. He is president of the international Catholic movement Vox Populi Mariae Mediatrici (Voice of the People for Mary Mediatrix). He is known for his international lectures in Mariology. He has addressed several episcopal conferences, including those of South India, Nigeria, Venezuela, and Costa Rica. In addition, he has served members of the episcopal hierarchy with preliminary investigations for reported apparitions and has made many conference appearances as well as several television appearances, for example, on EWTN and on Fox News.

Dr. Miravalle is a contributor to many theological anthologies and the author of numerous books, including Mary: Coredemptrix, Mediatrix, Advocate, which has been translated into fourteen languages, with over a half-million copies distributed worldwide, "With Jesus": The Story of Mary Co-redemptrix; The Marian Message to the Modern World; and The Seven Sorrows of China.

Sophia Institute

Sophia Institute is a nonprofit institution that seeks to nurture the spiritual, moral, and cultural life of souls and to spread the Gospel of Christ in conformity with the authentic teachings of the Roman Catholic Church.

Sophia Institute Press fulfills this mission by offering translations, reprints, and new publications that afford readers a rich source of the enduring wisdom of mankind.

Sophia Institute also operates two popular online Catholic resources: CrisisMagazine.com and CatholicExchange.com.

Crisis Magazine provides insightful cultural analysis that arms readers with the arguments necessary for navigating the ideological and theological minefields of the day. *Catholic Exchange* provides world news from a Catholic perspective as well as daily devotionals and articles that will help you to grow in holiness and live a life consistent with the teachings of the Church.

In 2013, Sophia Institute launched Sophia Institute for Teachers to renew and rebuild Catholic culture through service to Catholic education. With the goal of nurturing the spiritual, moral, and cultural life of souls, and an abiding respect for the role and work of teachers, we strive to provide materials and programs that are at once enlightening to the mind and ennobling to the heart; faithful and complete, as well as useful and practical.

Sophia Institute gratefully recognizes the Solidarity Association for preserving and encouraging the growth of our apostolate over the course of many years. Without their generous and timely support, this book would not be in your hands.

www.SophiaInstitute.com
www.CatholicExchange.com
www.CrisisMagazine.com
www.SophiaInstituteforTeachers.org

Sophia Institute Press® is a registered trademark of Sophia Institute.
Sophia Institute is a tax-exempt institution as defined by the
Internal Revenue Code, Section 501(c)(3). Tax I.D. 22-2548708.